ISBN 978-0-942702-66-8

© 2020 Rebecca McMahon Giles, PhD

Book design by Kaitlyn Nelsen and Stacy Hawthorne.
Editing by Tina Reeble and Erin Glenn.

Photos copyright © Adobe Stock, except the following:
© Rebecca Giles: pp. 11, 23, 25, 27, 29B, 56, 57, 58, 61B, 62, 64, 68, 69, 70, 77, 78, 82, 83, 85T, 87TR, 88, 89, 90B, 91, 93, 94, 99, 101-104, 108B, 110T, 113T, 117B, 119, 128, 174.
© Hattie Kingsley: pp. 44, 46, 61T, 112, 114.
Key: T (top) B (bottom) R (right) L (left)

This book may not be reproduced in whole or in part by any means without written permission of the publisher.

For more information about other Exchange Press publications and resources for directors and teachers, contact:

Exchange Press
7700 A Street
Lincoln, NE 68510
(800) 221-2864 • ExchangePress.com

A YOUNG WRITER'S WORLD

Creating Early Childhood Classrooms Where Authors Abound

Rebecca McMahon Giles, PhD

Exchange Press

TABLE OF CONTENTS

Introduction 6

Chapter 1: Setting the Stage 14

Chapter 2: Playing with Print 48

Chapter 3: Plenty of Print 72

Chapter 4: Publishing Possibilities 94

Chapter 5: Writing Role Models 122

Appendices 134

Notes 160

Bibliography 164

About the Author 174

INTRODUCTION

Immersing Young Children in Writing

"If people cannot write well, they cannot think well, and if they cannot think well, others will do their thinking for them."

—George Orwell

A Young Writer's World

The physical environment is a powerful tool to enhance children's experience with printed words.

Our surroundings affect our moods, our ability to form relationships, our effectiveness in work and play, and even our health. For young children, who are in a period of rapid brain development, the environment plays a substantial role in their growth and learning. This is particularly true in the areas of language and literacy acquisition. To a large extent, children's conceptual understanding of writing begins naturally through exposure to printed language in their environment. Children's awareness of writing is also influenced as they develop interest in language and a love of stories. By the time they begin walking and talking, surrounded by books and other print, and repeatedly hearing stories, songs, and poems, they become eager to record their own ideas in similar forms. With appropriate adult support, young children progress from orally playing with words to putting their words onto paper.

Purposeful opportunities to communicate through print help children build positive attitudes toward writing and about themselves as writers. As children explore the wonders of the written word, imitating the writers around them, they begin to realize that developing one's ideas on paper by composing sentences is a rewarding process. With plenty of time and rich experiences that allow children to incorporate writing into their play, they can successfully navigate the journey to become confident and creative authors.

This foundational process in early childhood development is imperative. The ability to express oneself in print, whether it is handwritten or typed, is a necessary educational skill and a talent highly valued in many ventures within classrooms, communities, and society. Writing is a means of communication that far exceeds the ability to form marks on paper. It is an expression of who we are as individuals and the primary means by which a child's intellect and academic success is evaluated. The focus of this book is creating classroom settings that foster children's ability to share thoughts and ideas on paper. This is not a manual on teaching handwriting. It is a guide to help you nurture children's writing as a means of communication.

Words and writing incorporated into various kinds of play help children learn language holistically.

A Young Writer's World

Children acquire written language in much the same way they learn to talk. When certain conditions are present, young children move from orally telling stories to putting their words onto paper. Australian educator, Brian Cambourne, identified these conditions (1988) after three years of observing and monitoring the language development of young children.[1] According to Cambourne, eight conditions combine to create the optimal environment for language learning, both oral and written: immersion, demonstration, engagement, expectation, responsibility, use, approximation, and response. In relation to young children becoming writers, Cambourne's theory can be summarized as follows:

> *Writing's value is communicated as children witness others engaged in writing and when children are provided access to supplies that promote writing on personally relevant topics in an authentic context in which to write. Children live up to the expectations that significant individuals hold for them and need adult acceptance of and response to their initial attempts to communicate in print.*

Each of Cambourne's conditions must be present in any classroom designed to facilitate and encourage children's writing development. While no single condition is more important, this book focuses on immersion. Immersion occurs when a child's surroundings are rich in written language. Saturating the environment with many different forms of relevant and appropriate print provides a strong foundation from which the other conditions can emerge. In such a classroom, the physical surroundings—adults, peers, furniture, supplies, equipment, activities, and displays—come together to facilitate children's continuous encounters with an abundance of print-related materials. To best support young authors, educators must intentionally immerse them in a writer's world.

Immersing Young Children in Writing

Writers, Authors and Publishing

Throughout this book, the term "publishing" includes any situation where authors share what they know with others through writing. In this definition, "writing" encompasses any and all means of written communication, such as dictation, drawing, and scribbling. The broad definition of publishing provided above was introduced in *Write Now! Publishing with Young Authors, PreK through Grade 2* (2007).[2] This definition of publishing differs from the more commonly accepted use of publishing as the final step in a long process, often involving revising and editing, when an author shares a polished piece of work deemed worthy of an audience. Instead, this definition of "publishing" acknowledges the author's willingness to have his work read. Simply stated, writing is published when others read it.

Written words are long-lasting. Their permanence often makes them the most effective means of communication, and any words written with the intention of being read by someone else have been "published." This comprehensive view of publishing is better suited to young children's egocentric nature and short attention spans. It also recognizes the digital communication so prevalent today, like text, email and Twitter posts, as publishing. Similarly, the "author" is the person or people who construct the message regardless of who produces the actual text; a story dictated by children and recorded in writing by the teacher was

Five-year-old Jay needed a grey marker to complete his picture. Over the course of several days, he repeatedly asked for the marker. When his verbal reminders failed to produce the desired outcome, Jay gave his mother a self-adhesive note that read "GRA MRKER." She soon delivered the marker, and Jay experienced first-hand the power of publishing!

A Young Writer's World

"written" by the children. As young children participate in abundant publishing opportunities, whether planned or spontaneous, individual or collaborative, on paper or electronic, the image of themselves as authors becomes firmly embedded.

The act of publishing for young children is two-fold. First, sharing what they have written provides motivation and recognition needed to sustain their interest in writing. Second, feedback from readers encourages and improves children's further attempts to write. As they interact with accomplished writers, they accumulate greater skill and begin to recognize the countless benefits of being able to communicate through print in thoughtful and creative ways. This will continue over time and lead to writing that is even more proficient in the future.

Young children gain valuable experience in programs that encourage them as authors. Obviously, children's knowledge and attitudes about writing will have a strong influence on the amount and quality of publishing that occurs in the classroom. The setting, however, can sway an individual for or against any endeavor, which makes it essential to consider how features of the classroom environment affect the writers it is intended to support. Environments that provide the time, materials, and challenges that allow children's development as authors to flourish must be intentionally planned.

A Young Writer's World will assist early childhood educators in creating preschool and kindergarten classrooms where children's thoughts and ideas take written form in a setting that encourages children to share their writing with others on a continual basis, rather than in rare moments. This book will guide and assist teachers, offering many suggestions to consider and customize to their own needs. Readers of *A Young Writer's World* are encouraged to adapt and personalize the information presented in response to their unique situations and specific students. Ultimately, the information will empower teachers to create early childhood classroom environments that engage and inspire young authors through a wonderful world of writing.

Each chapter addresses a specific aspect of the writing environment and provides suggestions to provoke consideration.

- **Chapter 1: Setting the Stage** describes classroom arrangement and set up strategies to support children's early attempts at writing. Nine learning centers – Art, Block, Computer, Fine Motor, Housekeeping, Library/Listening, Math, Publishing, and Science — are discussed, with a detailed focus on writing.

- **Chapter 2: Playing with Print** details desirable characteristics of print-related props and offers a variety of easy-to-implement suggestions for themed prop and discovery boxes to support dramatic play and scientific investigations. This chapter also includes a description of several educator techniques that support writing in the context of play.

- **Chapter 3: Plenty of Print** describes three types of print– books and other resources, environmental print, and purposeful print. Detailed examples illustrate ways to include each type of print in learning centers.

- **Chapter 4: Places to Publish** highlights the need for writers to become authors by making their work public and encourages the use of journals as a tool for daily writing experience. This chapter also provides readers with numerous options for displaying and publishing students' work in both traditional and innovative settings.

- **Chapter 5: Writing Role Models** emphasizes the need for parents and teachers to engage personally in the act of writing for many purposes in the presence of children.

CHAPTER ONE

Setting the Stage

"You don't write because you want to say something; you write because you've got something to say."

-F. Scott Fitzgerald

A Young Writer's World

Writing is a necessity within the teaching and learning process and should be a vital part of the daily routine in an early childhood classroom. You can accomplish this by encouraging children's voluntary and practical use of print as they comfortably communicate with teachers and classmates through writing. A positive experience sets the tone for future efforts and often leads to a desire to continue writing. It is essential that young children learn in a classroom that promotes and acknowledges their early attempts at writing, while providing numerous experiences worthy of recording in print. Although there is no single physical arrangement that best enhances writing development, an optimum classroom design presents writing and publishing as integral parts of the curriculum.

This chapter emphasizes the use of learning centers as the best means of expanding writing abilities by meeting the individual needs of children, as well as giving them responsibility for their own learning in a cooperative, secure setting.

When teachers incorporate print into all learning centers, children begin to understand that we live in language—spoken, heard, read, and written.

The Value of Learning Centers

Learning centers are "multipurpose areas within a classroom where equipment and materials are organized to promote active, child-centered learning."[1] Although learning happens throughout the classroom, the term *learning centers* connotes an arrangement where specific places in the classroom are organized and supplied to facilitate learning through exploration by individuals or in small groups. Learning centers provide a systematic way to manage space, materials, and time that is both efficient and versatile. Learning centers also provide an effective means of expanding children's abilities as authors, through publishing.

Learning centers hold many opportunities for publishing. Broadly defined, *publishing* is authors sharing what they know with others through any and all means of writing. Since all efforts to convey meaning on paper should be celebrated, dictated stories, scribbles, and strings of letters are acceptable forms of writing. Examples of publishing in learning centers would include scribbling a phone message in the housekeeping center or dictating the steps used to build a structure in the block center.

Writing is apparent in every aspect of real-life, and, therefore, easy to include in settings based on everyday experiences. Writing during center time allows children to imitate observed writing behaviors in meaningful and functional ways. When artificial and passive experiences such as the use of color pages and workbooks replace active learning through manipulating concrete objects and play, children have no opportunity to learn about the world around them. By contrast, learning centers supply real and engaging opportunities for children to learn about the world through interaction with materials and one another. Well-designed learning centers support the integrated nature of children's development and learning by awakening their senses, provoking curiosity, and stimulating their thinking.

A Young Writer's World

Support Vocabulary Development During Center Time Introduce terms such as density and buoyancy during a sink/float experiment or mention tint and shade while a child is painting at the easel. During play, when children use words like more/less, many/few, and heavy/light, which describe physical properties, conceptual knowledge and language is enhanced. Vocabularies flourish with the addition of context-specific words.

Preschoolers learn about language through play, using their play experiences as topics of conversations and stories. Similarly, children's time in learning centers provides the impetus for reading as well as the content for their discussions and writings. Center activities flow and take shape as children follow their own interests to create experiences worthy of recording. Children use these personally relevant and meaningful experiences to talk and write about.

Learning centers challenge children to accept and share responsibility for their own learning as they actively acquire, share, and explore concepts at their own pace. Children benefit from opportunities to work independently in a learning center and to work cooperatively with others, talking about the variety of approaches for accomplishing the same task or ways to write the same message.

Learning centers take optimum advantage of young children's natural abilities, interests, and enthusiasm for learning while meeting the individual needs of diverse learners. Young children learn almost exclusively by moving, playing, and doing. They actively construct knowledge by exploring the world around them during socially meaningful interactions. Learning centers provide organized areas that offer hands-on opportunities for individuals and small groups to test current understandings, discover new insights, and apply recently acquired skills.

Learning centers may be offered in all content areas and enhance development across all domains—social, emotional, physical, and cognitive. They provide necessary application of basic skills and previously introduced concepts while promoting the use of content-specific vocabulary and allowing opportunity for in-depth study. Learning centers also enable early childhood teachers to work with individuals or small groups while other children are actively engaged in a variety of self-selected, educationally beneficial activities.

Establishing Learning Centers

Whenever possible, involve children in constructing learning center rules, establishing procedural guidelines, and identifying suitable storage options. This involvement helps children develop planning and problem-solving skills, while generating feelings of ownership. Organize your centers to promote order and ease of cleanup. They do not need to be complex or expensive. Ideally, sharing your ideas and learning center materials with professional colleagues will save preparation time and enhance quality learning opportunities. Encourage both children and their families to contribute suggestions and materials for learning centers as well. Items found in nature, excess supplies from businesses, and recyclable items from home, which are available at little or no cost, add unique and interesting options.

Children take ownership and pride in organizing their learning center, during clean up time.

Objectives

Center activities can operate in one of two ways:
1. they can be structured experiences with a specific sequence of steps; or
2. they may be organized to provide open-ended exploration of materials.

While each approach offers particular benefits, both can increase conceptual understanding, stimulate creative thinking, promote oral language, and develop knowledge of print. Unrestricted activities like using a magnifying glass, pounding clay, rolling dough, creating a collage, putting puzzles together, scooping sand, building with blocks, or role-playing all reinforce the development of auditory, visual, and tactile experiences needed to successfully interact with books and print.

The nine centers discussed here are **Art, Block, Computer, Fine Motor, Housekeeping, Library/Listening, Math, Publishing,** and **Science**. To determine which learning centers to use, assess the needs of the children. Periodically rotate materials in your learning centers to sustain children's interest and maximize the use of limited space. **Appendix 1B Monthly Record of Child's Learning Center Participation** provides a checklist to track children's preferences by keeping a tally of the centers each child visits. Use information from the checklist to encourage children to try centers they do not typically choose or to make decisions regarding the need to alter available center choices.

For each learning center, you must be able to articulate key learning objectives and document children's progress toward meeting these objectives. Some objectives specific to writing are listed below.

Writing-Related Objectives Addressed in Learning Centers

With modeling and support, children will:
- Demonstrate an understanding of the structure and function of print.
- Show increasing awareness of books and print in the environment.
- Display growing interest and ability in writing.
- Experiment with a variety of writing tools.
- Demonstrate emerging knowledge of sound-symbol relationships (phonics) and familiarity with sight words.
- Discuss and respond to questions from others about their writing.
- Explore a variety of digital tools (e.g., computer, tablet, or smartboard) to create a piece of writing.
- Contribute personal opinions and/or factual information in shared writing activities.
- Use dictation and/or various forms of kid-writing for a variety of purposes (e.g., tell a story, express ideas, and share information.)
- Begin to incorporate basic punctuation when writing.

Signage

Once you have chosen the centers you will establish, determine where to locate each one in your classroom. To increase print and aid organization, consider center signs as a way to communicate physical location and specify learning goals. These signs provide children, parents, classroom volunteers, teaching assistants, administrators, and visitors with pertinent information.

In addition to signage that names and identifies the focus of each learning center, incorporate supplemental signs, charts, and labels to communicate the center's organizational system and established procedures, if necessary and appropriate. All of these written notifications are examples of purposeful print and can serve as beneficial models for children's own writing while they are in the center. Chapter 3 details more information on purposeful print in centers.

Materials

Learning center materials that support children as writers should span a wide range of possibilities. Before used independently, introduce materials and demonstrate how to use any equipment. **Appendix 2 Center Materials** lists materials for each center, selected based on their capacity for use by children of varying ages and abilities to meet multiple instructional purposes. As with the centers themselves, materials are offered intermittently and periodically rotated to maintain interest and, perhaps, to coordinate with a current theme of study.

> **Teacher Tip**
>
> **Use a Planning Chart for Play**
> Provide children with a simple chart using pictorial icons to represent the learning centers available. Children can use the chart when they have conversations about and record their daily plans for playing. Encourage children to draw and write their thoughts on the chart, expanding the benefits of planning their play.

A variety of materials helps children develop dexterity and creativity, and keep centers engaging.

A Young Writer's World

A well-stocked art center invites children to explore an endless variety of marks, artwork, and self-expression.

Art Center

The art center allows children to use various techniques and mediums as they engage in self-expression with an emphasis on the creative process rather than a finished product. Through experimentation, children begin to understand their world. They learn the value of visual representation and the meaning of symbolism. They practice how to control the assortment of tools they use. Creating art and writing are both means of recording a thought or idea, and both processes require the use of similar materials.

Writing thrives in a creative environment. Provide an abundant variety of materials for marking along with unique surfaces for drawing and writing to encourage children to experiment. The children will acquire new skills and abilities as they discover and explore different means of expressing themselves. Because art

Setting the Stage

Writing becomes a natural extension of artistic production when children are encouraged to sign and title their work.

experiences provide interesting writing topics, encourage children to try using a wide range of materials used in diverse ways. Occasions for publishing are a natural extension of artistic work when children are encouraged to provide a written description of their subject, list materials used, or outline the steps taken.

Four- and 5-year-olds learn to observe closely, think critically, and discuss respectfully when they are encouraged to look closely at classic works of art. As children engage in oral discussion related to both fine art examples and their own creations, you can introduce a wealth of art-related terms like collage, hue, sculptor, tint, and composition. The inclusion of art appreciation activities offers even more opportunities for children to publish as they evaluate fine art examples, describe master works, compare artists, contrast styles, or chronicle an artist's career.

Darius notes the color of paint used for his fish print.

Block Center

Block play enhances development of the whole child by improving physical, social, emotional, and cognitive abilities. As a result, its value in early childhood has long been recognized.

The block center provides children the opportunity to be active builders as they plan, construct, discuss, evaluate, demolish, and rebuild countless structures with a variety of building materials. Well-known for its mathematical benefits, this center also introduces crucial concepts needed for success in writing such as visual discrimination, use of abstract symbols, and language production. You can convert a basic block center to an optimum space for emerging and early authors by providing publishing opportunities within the context of construction play.

As children's block play becomes more complex, ideas and skills are integrated from various disciplines.

Students can "keep" their temporary block structures by recording their creations in a Block Journal.

Setting the Stage

Making a variety of writing tools, sign-making supplies, and building journals available in the block center will encourage frequent writing for varied purposes. A pocket chart with word cards or a dry-erase board with markers provides a temporary option for planning what to build or recording work that has already taken place. Print can also be used to communicate a child's desire to continue their block play later, by making and displaying signs such as "work in progress" or "under construction."

A block journal is highly recommended. A single, community block journal or individual building journals for each child allow children to record experiences related to their building.

These journals, which contain photographs or illustrations along with child-produced or dictated text, provide a place to permanently record children's temporary creations. Chapter 2 provides a detailed example of one preschooler's experience using a block journal.

When Bryson realized that center time was ending and he had not yet finished his construction project, Ms. Adams suggested that he make a sign letting the other children know that it was not to be dismantled during clean-up. His "do not touch" sign clearly communicated his desire that his structure remain undisturbed.

A Young Writer's World

Developmentally appropriate software enhances children's experience of early literacy. Nico listens to a story and watches the words on the screen at the same time.

Computer Center

The computer center is a unique and substantial contribution to young children's learning and development. Access to a computer and developmentally appropriate software can increase creativity, improve communication skills, and foster academic growth while improving eye-hand coordination, increasing motivation to learn, and supporting childrens' confidence in using technology. There are numerous software options and internet sites available to assist children in gaining the knowledge and skills needed to read and write. They also experience perseverance to achieve goals, since many computer activities are designed to encourage finishing sequential tasks, unlocking levels, or winning a game.

Setting the Stage

During center time, Madison eagerly awaited her turn at the computer. While waiting, she created the journal entry shown here. After writing her first name and last initial, she date stamped the page. Then she drew herself at the computer, added a color picture on the monitor, and used the nearby center sign as a model to label her picture.

A computer, however, should not be used as an electronic workbook where children operate repetitive drill-and-practice programs or used as a reward for good behavior. Instead, a computer or other technological devices should be one of many materials available for children to explore and use as a tool for increasing general knowledge, language abilities, social competence, and writing skills.

Computers provide a means for children to revise, edit, illustrate, and save their final versions of original compositions in a wide range of formats. In addition, a computer and the time spent in this center may also lead to interest in new topics and an excitement for writing in traditional formats.

Using the internet to extend publishing opportunities with the element of a cyber audience through email and online publishing is discussed further in Chapter 4.

Use your Computer for Audio Books

- Use an iPad app such as Record Box to create an audio file during story time. Then, transfer the file to the classroom computer for children's use.

- At StoryNory (storynory.com) children can find original and classic stories, poems, myths, and fairytales accompanied by a written account of the audio, which allows children to read along or reread favorite parts.

- Storyline Online (storylineonline.net) provides video of a celebrity reading supplemented with views of illustrations from the actual book.

A Young Writer's World

Incorporating opportunities for writing into every Learning Center helps children see that we live in words. Everyone writes, every day.

Housekeeping Center

Dramatic play, also called pretend play, involves children acting out real-world situations and taking on the roles of different people or characters as they explore items and tools adults use in everyday life. In an early childhood classroom, the area devoted to dramatic play is traditionally known as the housekeeping or home center. In this center, children enact ideas and experiment with props as they dramatize both familiar and novel situations. Cognitive and social development are enhanced in this setting, which encourages cooperation, requires peer interaction, fosters perspective-taking, and stretches the imagination through pretend play. Children apply their knowledge of language, numbers, and print in real life situations as they

Setting the Stage

Opportunities for list-making in the housekeeping area—what does the baby need? What is the baby's name?

recreate scenes and participate in role-play related to well-known locations such as the home, grocery store, or doctor's office. The presence of print-related props promotes reading and writing in children's dramatic play while creating numerous publishing opportunities as they pretend to take phone messages, write shopping lists, and record a patient's symptoms.

More on the use of props to support pretend play, writing and publishing in the housekeeping area is detailed in Chapter 2.

Converting the housekeeping center to a workshop provided the opportunity for Padraic to take an order for a custom-built table.

29

A Young writer's world

A variety of appropriate loose parts materials invite children to explore.

Fine Motor Center

Fine motor development progresses slowly during the preschool years. Young children lack sophisticated manual dexterity and can become frustrated when expected to perform tasks that require the precise use of hand muscles or meticulous eye-hand coordination. Providing a number of varied opportunities for children to use hands and fingers and practice fine motor skills promotes development. Despite children's advanced abilities to operate an assortment of electronic devices, traditional manipulative activities such as putting pegs in pegboards, stringing beads, and working puzzles are as important as ever for increasing tactile awareness and developing children's ability to grasp, release, insert, turn, and twist objects.

Sorting, collecting, combining, and arranging all help build dexterity and focus.

Setting the Stage

> **Teacher Tip**
>
> **Create Opportunities to Encourage Fine Motor Development**
>
> - Provide spray water bottles to care for plants or create sidewalk art.
> - Place child-safe tweezers or tongs, small malleable items (sponge pieces or pom-poms) and numbered sorting containers (ice cube trays or muffin tins) in the math center.
> - Provide spring-loaded clothespins in the housekeeping center to hang doll clothes and costumes or in the science center to sequence picture cards on a line.
> - Add small child-sized paper punches to the art center.
> - Provide small tops to spin in the fine motor area.
> - Display cards, coins, or buttons on the floor, and encourage children to turn them over.
> - Put a manual eggbeater in the water table to create bubbles with dish washing liquid.
> - Provide plastic eyedroppers for art projects or science experiments.
> - Place finger puppets in the library/listening center.

Remember, fine motor development is by no means limited to the fine motor center. Fine motor skills are also refined as children paint at an easel or dress in costumes for dramatic play. As you provide encouragement, and assistance when needed, children will strengthen and develop muscles in their fingers and hands. Designating a specific center in your classroom focused on fine motor development simply ensures children will regularly have access to beneficial tools, toys, and materials.

Print-related manipulative materials allow children to develop their knowledge of letters and words along with their fine-motor skills.

As in other developmental areas, children's level of proficiency with fine motor tasks varies and can be influenced by numerous factors including culture and gender. To avoid feelings of inadequacy and stress, acknowledge what children can do and encourage their willingness to try new activities.

A Young Writer's World

Carlo combines letter shapes with images as he paints.

Children can grab and hold markers however it is comfortable for them, to keep creating freely.

When children do show an interest in writing and begin to make letter-like shapes, allow them to experiment with how letters are formed to gain confidence in expressing themselves with print. By four years of age, many children hold a crayon or pencil pinched between the thumb and index finger, using an adult-like grasp sometimes referred to as a tripod or mature pencil grasp. This grasp is preferred because it offers the greatest amount of control over the writing tool and is the least fatiguing method for the muscles in the arm and hand. When children hold a writing tool in a closed-fist grasp, it may indicate that they are lacking fine motor skills.

Instead of forcing a child into a tripod grasp, intentionally embed increased fine motor development opportunities into the daily routine so there is further opportunity to develop the muscles in their hands. If an

Setting the Stage

interested and persistent child is having trouble writing, you may step in and demonstrate a simpler way to form a specific letter or offer informal assistance.

Formal handwriting instruction such as repetitive tracing or forming letters is not needed since handwriting is best practiced within the context of real writing experiences.

Brianna uses her finger to make a heart in salt.

Teacher Tip

Provide Appropriate Practice Writing Letters

Tactile Trays - Place a small amount of salt, flour, sand, finger paint, or shaving cream on a cookie sheet or colored tray to provide an alternative medium for beginning writers. Children can make letters and words using fingers, brushes, or sticks. They can also erase written messages quickly and easily, allowing for multiple attempts and quick revisions.

Plastic Bag Writing Tablets - Use packing or duct tape to seal non-toxic finger paint or hair gel inside a clear plastic sandwich bag with all the air removed to create a sensory writing experience. Offer tools such as a craft stick or cotton swab.

A Young Writer's World

Library/Listening Center

Children need to hear and read many stories before they can write their own, which makes the classroom library/listening center a priority. A varied collection of interesting literature, audio books, and related props provides children with immediate access to stories and information. Time spent in the library/listening center will foster oral language, enhance comprehension, develop children's print knowledge, instill a love of books, and increase awareness of writing forms, while providing writing models and an understanding of authorship.

An appealing area containing books where children can read or listen to audio recordings in a relaxed, comfortable manner encourages written language development. Every classroom needs a variety of trade books. You can share from your own collection, request donations from parents and community members, or borrow books from your school and public libraries for children to use.

Make Your Book Collection Language-Rich
Exposing children to various English dialects and languages other than English through literature increases children's awareness of the diversity of both the people and languages that comprise our world.

Consider options to organize and display books where children can easily access them. Include bookshelves that show only the spines to maximize space, as well as shelving that allows you to display front covers to entice reading. Arranging books by subject or type makes them easy to locate. Book baskets offer an organizational option that allows children to flip quickly through selections separated into categories of interest.

> **Teacher Tip**
>
> **Encouraging Standard English**
> Hearing, discussing, and dramatizing stories written in Standard English aids children in adopting correct language for personal use and is preferable to constant verbal correction, which can be interpreted as judgmental and critical.

Clearly labeled book baskets ensure that Ryan can find his favorite stories in the library/listening center.

Prominently display seasonal, theme or author-related books, and rotate the selection periodically to generate interest. Posters and/or bulletin boards that encourage reading or depict information about authors and their books can also be displayed as sources of inspiration.

An inviting, well-stocked library/listening center results in an increased level of voluntary interaction with books. Carefully select center materials to support children's involvement in literacy events. Whether self-initiated or teacher-prompted, alone or in small groups, such events facilitate children's interest in books and encourage appropriate book-handling skills. Audio books can be used to supplement children's experiences by providing an engaging format to hear a text repeatedly. When children hear the same book multiple times, they become more aware of the

> **Teacher Tip**
>
> **Literature Prop Ideas**
>
> 1. Kiz Club (kizclub.com/stories.htm) provides free story pieces to accompany many favorite books including *Brown Bear Brown Bear*, *Pete the Cat*, *The Mitten*, and, *Silly Sally*. Download the pictures in color or black and white, print on cardstock, cut out, and attach to wooden dowels or paint stirrers to make stick puppets. For use with a flannel board, attach a piece of felt to the back of each prop.
> 2. Photos are an easy-to-make prop for any book. Simply use your phone or tablet to take photos of different illustrations in the book, which does not violate copyright unless the pictures are distributed or sold. Display the images on an interactive white board or print for students to sequence in correct order and then retell the story from those photos.

Puppets give students a fun way to retell their favorite stories, and create their own as well.

pattern and rhythm of text, become familiar and comfortable with a greater number of words, and increase their depth of understanding as they acquire additional details.

You may choose to provide literature props such as puppets and felt-board stories to encourage children to retell the stories they have repeatedly heard read to them.

When children orally retell a familiar story, they begin to develop a sense of story (setting, characters, and plot), better understand sequence (beginning, middle and end), and gain expressive vocabulary. Using puppets or other storytelling props is an easy and fun way to make retelling stories more interactive. As children become proficient in retelling a particular story, you can enrich the experience further by encouraging children to add details to the story or use a different voice for each character. Publishing children's retellings is discussed in Chapter 4.

Setting the Stage

Math Center

Mathematics helps young children make sense of their world outside of school and helps them construct a solid foundation for academic success.[2] Young children learn math slowly through repeated exposure. They do not learn much math that is not "real." Rather, they gain an initial understanding of mathematics as they sort objects, compare quantities, notice shapes, and recognize patterns during play ("We need a different block. This one is too long.") and routine daily activities. ("He got three crackers for snack, and I only got two.") Children need many experiences that help them relate the intuitive knowledge of mathematics acquired naturally to the specific vocabulary and conceptual frameworks of the discipline.

Repeated interaction with certain manipulatives increases familiarity and brings confidence.

A Young Writer's World

Seeing, holding and tracing geometric shapes connects math, art and writing.

Students gravitate to their favorite tools for learning and play. Kaia loves the abacus!

In high-quality programs, 3- to 6-year-olds are actively introduced to mathematical concepts, methods, and language through a range of hands-on experiences. They are provided guided opportunities to recognize, reinvent, reorganize, quantify, generalize, and refine their understandings of numbers, geometry, measurement, and numeric operations using concrete objects.

Setting the Stage

Using manipulatives offers the following benefits for children:
- develops early numeracy concepts;
- offers direct experiences with basic attributes of color, size, and shape;
- provides opportunities for cooperative problem-solving; and
- increases awareness of cultural diversity.

With recurring practice, children's confidence, competence, and interest in mathematics flourish and they move from physical to symbolic representations of mathematics as they begin to express their thinking with pictures. The transition from pictures to more abstract mathematical symbols will come easily for some children and take a longer time for others. To facilitate the use of abstract symbols to express themselves mathematically, having children explain their ideas using models with pictorial and/or symbolic representations is essential. Children's ability to abstractly represent, communicate, and connect mathematical ideas will continue to improve when meaningful symbolic experiences are connected to prior knowledge and build on children's individual backgrounds.

Seeing numbers in different contexts in the math center, makes numbers familiar to children.

Opportunities for publishing in math evolve from children's exploration and discovery as they use writing to clarify and share their new understandings. Counting books, number rhymes, math journals, story problems, and math dictionaries are just a few of the writing formats that are possible in the math center.

A Young Writer's World

Dalton and Joey work at the publishing center to record their stories in blank books.

Publishing Center

Once children personally begin to experience the pleasure of writing and their efforts are acknowledged, they become motivated to write more. In addition to providing a print-rich environment and supplies for recording language throughout the classroom, designate a space specifically for use by young writers who want to sharpen their skills and improve their craft. Writing occurs in all centers, but the publishing center provides easy access to an abundant variety of writing materials as well as tools to assist children in writing independently. Keep materials well organized and clearly labeled to facilitate children's self-selection of supplies. Furnishings that support seated work are appropriate but not required. Be careful not to convey the erroneous message that writing only takes place when seated at a table. Instead, establish the primary purpose of the publishing center as a repository for all things needed to produce a written message.

Setting the Stage

Publishing center materials fit into four basic categories: writing instruments, writing surfaces, book-making supplies, and writing tools.

- **Writing instruments** are any items used to produce marks on paper or other surfaces and range from crayons and pencils to Bingo markers. The options for writing instruments should vary in size and shape allowing each child to choose the instrument most comfortable in his/her hand and best suited for the specific writing task.

- **Writing surfaces** mainly consist of different sizes, shapes, colors, and thicknesses of paper but can also include cardboard pieces, individual dry erase boards, various notepads, and pre-made blank books. Clipboards and student journals are a must. Clipboards offer the portability needed to write in numerous locations both inside the classroom and out, while providing a child-friendly, informal format for writing. Children's daily journals, discussed further in Chapter 4, can be conveniently stored in the publishing center.

- **Book-making supplies** include items for covers, like wallpaper samples, thin pieces of cardboard from discarded gift boxes or pages from an expired wall calendar, as well as materials to offer a selection of binding options such as brads, staples, and string.

- **Writing tools** range from letter stamps and stickers to picture dictionaries and word charts.

Some items overlap categories. For example, colored construction paper or thin cardboard pieces might be a writing surface as well as a book cover. As with all centers, rotate items in and out of the publishing center at various points to maintain interest and offer constant variety. Be sure items in each category are always available.

A Young Writer's World

Involving children in organizing the Science Center will increase their engagement and allow them to help at clean up time.

Science Center

The science center enhances children's acquisition of cognitive process skills as they investigate relationships and apply problem-solving strategies to learn about themselves, others, and the world. A well-equipped science center contains materials that require looking, probing, touching, and all types of sensory exploration. You can stock the science center with naturally occurring phenomena from nature for children to observe, explore, research, and share. Promote scientific investigation with additional collections of supplies organized and stored as discovery boxes, including books, writing materials, and items related to a specific topic. Chapter 2 provides examples of discovery boxes. As children investigate a topic of interest, they speak, listen, read, and write to construct their own meanings and share their findings. As a result, their language and literacy skills advance along with their general knowledge.

Young children are innately curious and often possess unending questions regarding how the world works. Satisfying this curiosity becomes the impetus for writing in the science center as children compose stories, make charts, record data, and create books to

Setting the Stage

communicate what they know, want to know, and have learned about their world through observing, organizing, describing, questioning, and searching for answers.

Scientists often document their observations and findings in a notebook or journal. Encourage children to record information through written text or visual representation using pictures, symbols, charts or graphs. As authors publishing their stories, young scientists use writing to report what they discovered through their experimentation.

Labeling parts of plants, animals and flowers brings print into the classroom.

45

Evaluating the Writing Environment

Classroom environments that promote and support writing can vary greatly and use any combination of recommended characteristics. **Appendix 3 The Writing Environment Checklist** provides a quick, easy guide for assessing a classroom's writing potential. Use the checklist to evaluate each of the nine learning centers described in this chapter along with five general classroom features:

- books and other reading materials;
- supplies and equipment for recording language;
- children's work displays;
- written information; and
- signs, labels, and directions.

Responding to the series of "yes" or "no" questions will provide insight into ways you might increase environmental factors that promote children's writing development.

Bringing letters and written words into your learning space can be its own creative expression.

Conclusion

All centers promote writing development when they contain print-related materials for independent inquiry during play. You can best facilitate children's literacy learning through play by making a wide variety of reading and writing tools available throughout your classroom. Stock learning centers with materials that encourage communication through print and promote publishing. Provide opportunities for children to explore the functions and features of print as they reenact previously observed writing behaviors.

CHAPTER TWO

Playing with Print

> "Writing comes more easily if you have something to say."
>
> —Sholem Asch

Across all ages, abilities, and cultures, a unique set of attributes identify play. Play is intrinsically motivated, process oriented, non-literal, active and governed by parameters agreed upon by the players. Play largely encompasses any of a wide variety of behaviors through which children attempt to discover who they are and what they can do. Through this process, children also learn about the world around them.

Pretend play supports children's language acquisition and expression.

A substantial body of research suggests a strong relationship between play and the cognitive, physical, social, emotional, behavioral, and language development of young children. For instance, the research and philosophies of several eminent child development theorists and educators, including Jean Piaget, Lev Vygotsky, Maria Montessori, Friedrich Froebel, and John Dewey, advocate the importance of play for growth and development. Their combined bodies of work and subsequent conclusions serve as the fundamental guiding principles in support of play as a child's major way of learning. Contrary to a frivolous pursuit, play is an outlet for children to explore their ideas, feelings, social relationships, curiosity, imagination, and autonomy.

One noted and significant benefit of play is its contribution to children's acquisition of language. Aspects of play that contribute to language development include the inherent social interaction, the volume of language production, high levels of engagement, and opportunities to practice forming symbolic relationships. Thus, time spent playing provides valuable opportunities for language learning. When considered expansively, oral language consists of phonology, grammar, morphology, vocabulary, discourse, and pragmatics. Since this is also the knowledge needed for word recognition and comprehension, oral language proficiency contributes to reading and writing abilities. Basically, young children use the language knowledge they have acquired through speaking and listening and apply it to text.

Listening and engaging with children during pretend play encourages them to express their thoughts and actions with words.

Understanding the Relationship between Play and Literacy

- Play, as a fundamental cognitive activity, is preparation for more complex cognitive activities, such as reading and writing.

- Representational abilities acquired when pretending ("this stands for that") transfer to written language.

- When children engage in play experiences with print-related materials, their actions include literacy skills.

Pretend or dramatic play, because of its inherent symbolism, has a strong connection with literacy. When pretending, children mentally allow one object to represent another. For example, a child holds a block to her ear and has a one-sided conversation with her grandmother. In this situation, the block has become a symbol for

A Young Writer's World

Give children plenty of time in their play, to go deeply into letters, numbers and symbols.

a phone. A child's pretending is an expression of abstract thought that evidences a beginning ability to use symbols, which is necessary for reading and writing. All three activities—pretending, reading, and writing—require the ability to use objects (or pictures of them), words, and mental images to stand for actual items, events, or actions.

To fully benefit children's writing development, play requires
1. an interesting, well-organized environment,
2. ample time for children to be deeply engaged, and
3. teachers who act as facilitators and coaches as children play.

This chapter details how children's engagement in pretend play and scientific investigation supports their language and literacy development and ways you can promote publishing for many, varied purposes through these activities.

As the teacher facilitates discussion, children place their letters on a letter tree.

Writing Development

Learning to write can be as natural for a child as learning to talk, run, or sing. Children's writing awareness begins very young, and their initial attempts at writing occur long before they fully understand symbolism or represent their ideas using standard forms. As children make connections between spoken and written language, they extend their understanding of oral language when they attempt to capture speech on paper. This progression moves from their preliterate use of pictures and scribbles to an increased awareness of print expressed with the use of marks resembling letters or random letter strings. With an increased understanding of print concepts and sound-symbol relationships, children transition to using invented and conventional spelling. More information regarding kid-writing, including examples of various forms, is provided in Chapter 4.

Over time, pictures and scribbles begin to include letter shapes and letter strings.

While presented in a continuum, writing development is fluid rather than strictly sequential. Children use various forms at different times or even combine forms depending on such factors as their purpose for writing, intended audience, and level of support. Further, children's writing development is strongly influenced by both individual and cultural variations. Regardless of a child's emerging skill level, writing development is enhanced in an environment created to immerse children in opportunities to communicate through print.

A Young Writer's World

Teacher Tip

Pretending builds children's writing skills through opportunities to:

- imitate adult writing behaviors observed in books, on television, or in person,

- recognize that different tasks require different types of writing, and

- produce a wide variety of print.

The Connection Between Pretending and Writing

Children's literacy development is "a dynamic, developmental process involving language, thought, and social interaction."[1] Children's pretend play typically begins about age three or four and evolves as they mature, with the ability to organize other children for role-play independently appearing around five years of age. When pretending, children project a mental representation onto reality. When pretending with others, the activity involves thinking, communicating, and interacting socially.

Five- to 7-year-olds possess advanced language functions and perspective that allow them to often invent and enact elaborate stories. This process expands their creative thinking abilities and improves memory as they recall details from events similar to those recreated as well as the sequence of actions performed. As children make-believe with peers, they practice conflict resolution as they negotiate roles and learn to think widely when searching for solutions to problems or practice imagining alternate endings.

Problem-solving and cooperation in dramatic play foster language development and imagination.

Research Highlights

Initial interest in a play-literacy connection appeared in the 1970s and surged during the 1990s. Increased popularity of play and literacy as a research topic most likely resulted from new insights into the development of foundational literacy during early childhood. Through this research, a positive relationship between the play environment—both physical and social—and early literacy activity and skills has been documented.

- More literacy behaviors occur in play areas equipped with thematically chosen literacy materials than in classrooms without such materials.[2]
- Adding literacy props to the play areas in a kindergarten classroom greatly increased the amount of time children engaged in literate behaviors during play.[3]
- A greater number of literacy demonstrations occur when paper, pencils, note pads, books, magazines, signs, stationary, and other print-rich props are included in the dramatic play center.[4]
- Specific situational contexts with corresponding props result in more complex literacy activities.[5]
- Children's reading and writing becomes more purposeful in literacy-enriched play environments.[6]
- Literacy props added to the block play area prompt numerous literacy events.[7]
- A sense of collaboration and cooperation exists within literate play, and the availability and authenticity of the literacy materials seems to play a role in the success of maintaining the play theme.[8]
- Three-year-old children's level of pretend skill (symbolic play) predicted their emergent writing status.[9]
- Children use a variety of strategies, such as negotiating and coaching, to help each other learn about literacy during play.[10]
- A teacher's participation in guided play is pivotal in helping children incorporate literacy materials into their imaginative play.[11]

A Young Writer's World

Promoting Publishing in Pretend Play

As discussed in Chapter 1, children's writing development is fully supported in developmentally appropriate ways when the environment is used as a vehicle for learning. Environments with writing-related props can nurture young children's interest and abilities in writing during play as they practice the act of writing in the context of pretending.

As children act out personal experiences or familiar stories in settings free of pressure and predetermined expectations, they experiment using print for a variety of real-life purposes.

Begin by integrating writing-related props into pretend play to increase the quantity and depth of literacy behaviors that occur during play and facilitate gains in young children's knowledge about the functions of writing.

You can also enhance children's language and literacy development with props used to create novel scenarios. As children interact with unusual props and take on different roles, they try out new words and expressions through rich collaborative dialogues and discover new reasons to write.

Converting a center's traditional setting into a fresh context creates numerous new opportunities for both pretending and

A notepad and pencil on the telephone tray in this Montessori classroom are examples of appropriate, authentic, and functional props for three-year-old Lucas. The presence of these items prompted him to take a message after ending his call.

publishing. For example, children working as florists might use kid-writing when designing and listing prices for a bouquet while children portraying customers personalize small floral enclosure cards. The selection of pretend play themes can come from topics of study, personal experiences or well-known stories. Themes often emerge because of children's interest and remain until attention begins to fade, usually about two weeks. See **Appendix 4 Scenarios and Props** for ideas related to realistic settings, such as a pizzeria or car dealership.

During a thematic unit on community helpers, Mrs. Morris converted her publishing center into a post office to promote letter writing.

Pretend Play in Novel Scenarios

- Enhances concept development.
- Assists in differentiating between fantasy and reality.
- Builds expressive language skills.
- Facilitates mastery of grammar.
- Strengthens comprehension of the pragmatics of language.
- Introduces new vocabulary.
- Furthers understanding of symbols.
- Increases awareness of reading and writing in real world situations.

A Young Writer's World

Teacher Tip

Identifying Symbolic Props
Provide a few props for a new pretend play scenario, such as a white coat and stuffed animals for a veterinarian's office. Then, challenge children to locate items around the room that can be repurposed as symbolic props, like the plastic storage baskets in blocks for pet kennels.

Introducing a new area or context for pretend play gives children an invitation to use language differently.

Creating the scenario does not ensure that children will know how to play the roles. Even when children play in a theme that you expect is familiar, like restaurant or grocery store, they may revert to established roles as parents and children because this is most familiar. Try using books to increase children's familiarity with realistic settings. Books can also be used to vary pretend play with themes inspired by well-loved characters or favorite stories. While realistic fiction and information books are best for encouraging play in real-world settings, the unrestricted possibilities and diverse language in fantasy stories and fairy tales provide the best opportunity for learning new words.

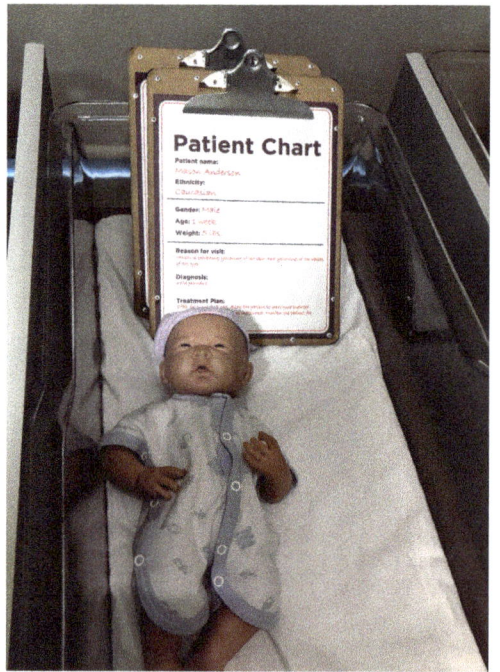

When introducing a new context, begin by naming and explaining the props.

"This is a stethoscope. Doctors and nurses use it to listen to a patient's heartbeat. Like this."

When you do this, you are providing the vocabulary needed for children's future interaction with the physical objects. Identifying props and the actions that accompany them models how to communicate ideas about play to friends.

"Here. You use the stethoscope to listen to the baby's heart."

Realistic props are useful tools to introduce children to pretend play. They help children maintain their roles and remember what

Types of Props

- **Realistic** – actual objects
  Example: surgical mask and gauze
- **Symbolic** – using an object in place of something else
  Example: drum mallet for a microphone and side-by-side chairs for a car
- **Open-ended** – unstructured and multi-functional items
  Example: cardboard boxes and pieces of cloth

the play scenario is all about ("I'm wearing an apron and hat because I'm the chef.") Realistic props, however, limit children's symbolic representation, which occurs when they use objects to represent other objects. For best results, provide realistic props in combination with other types of props.

You can model and encourage symbolic thinking when you demonstrate how a single prop can be used in multiple ways. For example, a plastic plate previously used realistically in a restaurant scenario can become a steering wheel in the auto shop.

While props need to be largely realistic at first, the ratio of realistic to symbolic props can gradually increase as you note developmental skills becoming more sophisticated. With time, experience, and adult guidance, children learn to use open-ended materials for their props, make their own props, or even pretend that they have a prop when they do not.

Teacher Tip

Vocabulary Development During Pretend Play Because children are most likely to learn new words during authentic conversations about something that interests them, use specific terminology when talking to children about their play. A well-developed vocabulary helps children produce writing that is clear and succinct ("equipment" rather than "stuff a firefighter uses to put out fires").

A Young Writer's World

A science or nature journal encourages children to observe and record what they see outside, possibly including weather words introduced in the classroom.

Promoting Publishing During Scientific Investigations

Children are natural scientists. Their innate sense of curiosity propels their constant questioning as they search for answers to "how" and "why" things work. As children move into the preschool years, they take on a more active role in searching out, describing, and explaining events that occur in the physical and natural world. Scientific investigations provide a valuable avenue for helping young children become authors as they use writing to collect data and share discoveries. Trade books provide print models and support each phase of an investigation by introducing, clarifying, and extending concepts.

Playing with Print

The term "heuristic play" was coined by child psychologist Elinor Goldschmeid to describe the exploratory process babies and toddlers employ as they use all their senses to discover the properties of objects. "Put simply, it consists of offering a group of children, for a defined period of time in a controlled environment, a large number of objects and receptacles with which they play freely without adult intervention." Heuristic play is about curiosity and exploration as children select, manipulate, study, and compare objects to determine what the objects can and cannot do.[12]

When applied to young children in early childhood settings, you can support the ideas behind heuristic play by organizing supplies into "discovery boxes." Each discovery box holds a collection of natural, found, or recycled objects and related materials that are associated with a particular theme, like magnets, reflection, seeds and measurement. **Appendix 5 Discovery Boxes by Theme** offers a variety of options to try.

Loose pieces and parts fascinate children as they combine and use them in a variety of ways.

Discovery Boxes surprise children with a theme, and new possibilities to explore.

A Young Writer's World

After observing the painted lady butterfly caterpillars in Mrs. Schultz's kindergarten class, children document their observations in their "Butterfly Journals."

Discovery boxes support inquiry using the scientific process while children determine how items are used.

Steps in the Scientific Process
1. Ask a question.
2. Do background research.
3. Construct a hypothesis.
4. Test your hypothesis by doing an experiment.
5. Analyze the data and draw a conclusion.
6. Share results.

Discovery boxes stimulate children's examination of common objects and inspire them to create written records of their research, data collection, and findings.

Include three types of items in each discovery box:
1. objects inviting hands-on exploration,
2. informative children's literature, and
3. writing materials.

Playing with Print

In addition to the collection of items and books related to the theme, each discovery box should contain an enticing way for children to communicate their discoveries and new understandings. For example, pair one or more writing utensils with a place for recording results. The chart below provides some suggestions:

Writing Utensils	Places for Recording Results
Pencils	Blank book(s)
Assorted ink pens	Journals
Colored markers *(thick and thin)*	Small notepads
Scented markers	Clipboards with paper
Colored pencils	Sorting charts
Crayons	Blank bar graphs
Letter stamps and stamp pads	Graph paper
White and colored chalk	Typing paper *(white and multi-colored)*
	Construction paper *(white and multi-colored)*
	Assorted lined paper
	Stationary
	Index cards
	Self-adhesive note pads
	Steno or legal pads
	Accounting ledgers
	Composition books

A Young Writer's World

Ms. Hegwood helps Martin brainstorm ideas for the title of the book he is writing in the publishing center.

Adult Guidance and Support

Children are naturally interested in the world around them, and a variety of print-related props and materials enrich play environments. Becoming an author, however, does not happen through osmosis. While playing independently in the block center, children can learn that a tower tumbles if built on an unsteady base. On the other hand, literacy concepts, skills, and understandings are taught. They must be *learned from someone else*. Hence, Cambourne's requirement of demonstration and response as conditions for learning language.[13]

Children will not learn sound-symbol relationships if they haven't been shown a letter while hearing the letter's sound being made. Children won't learn that letters and words are formed from left to right unless they observe someone writing, and children won't know the dot at the end of a statement is called a period and means stop unless they are told. Interaction between adults and knowledgeable peers is needed for literacy learning to occur.

The conversation below illustrates how a group of children practiced using letter names and sounds during sandbox play on a preschool playground. Prior to this exchange, the teacher used a permanent marker to write the first letter of each animal's name on assorted plastic animals and placed them in the sand with several small shovels.

Children observe and imitate the writing behaviors of adults in their environment.

> **Teacher** *(when Isabella uncovered a bear in the sand)*: "What can you tell me about that animal?"
>
> **Isabella:** "It's a bear!"
>
> **Jeremiah** *(pointing to letter)*: "There's a B on it's stomach, b-b-bear!"
>
> **Alice** *(approaching the sandbox)*: "What's in here?"
>
> **Jeremiah:** "Animals with letters."
>
> **Teacher to Alice:** "Would you like to dig to find the animals?"
>
> **Alice** *(after digging)*: "I got a turtle!"
>
> **Jeremiah** *(pointing to the animal)*: "Yeah 'T' for turtle!"

Such interactions add to children's growing understanding of phonetic knowledge, which in turn, contributes to their developing ability to communicate in print.

A Young Writer's World

Watching and listening intently to children before responding supports their self-directed learning.

For a print-rich environment to fully benefit children, the social aspect of the environment must be considered along with the selection and arrangement of materials. A carefully prepared environment coupled with modeling by and encouragement from others changes visual exposure to print into meaningful interaction with it. Establishing a challenging and intriguing setting packed with print and opportunities to publish in meaningful ways is only the first step. As the teacher, you are needed to offer assistance and make suggestions while ensuring that the activities remain self-initiated and child-directed. The goal for integrating literacy learning into play is to balance active support with respect for a child's level of interest, skill, and conceptual understanding. The key to meeting this goal is sensitive adult guidance.

Vygotsky referred to the process of providing adult support for the purpose of extending a child's learning beyond their current abilities as scaffolding. This adult guidance and support can occur through both verbal exchanges and modeling.[14]

Verbal Prompting

A verbal exchange can be an especially effective means for supporting children's literacy development as language is used to coach children beyond their initial range of possibility. Consider how verbal prompting assisted Tyler in phonetically spelling a desired word in the following exchange:

Tyler *(bringing his picture and sitting down beside his teacher):* "How do you spell football? I already have the F."

Teacher: "Listen while I say football slowly stretching out the word. f-ooo-t-b-aaa-lll. What sound do you hear after f?"

Tyler: "I hear t" *(makes T on paper after F)*

Teacher: "Listen again. f-ooo-t-b-aaa-lll. Do you hear any other sounds?"

Tyler *(imitating teacher):* "f-ooo-t-b-aaa-lll, I hear b."

Teacher: "What letter makes the b sound?"

Tyler *(making B on his paper):* "B"

Teacher: "f-ooo-t-b-aaa-lll. The last sound is l-l. Do you know what letter makes the l-l-l sound?" *(Tyler shakes his head no.)* L-l-lion. Can you find the picture of the lion on our alphabet chart?"

Tyler leaves the table, goes to the alphabet chart hanging on the wall, copies the letter L on his paper, and returns to the table.

Teacher *(as Tyler points to the letter L he wrote):* "Yes. That's an L. The letter L makes the l-l-l sound. *(Moving her pointer finger from left to right under the four letters Tyler has written)* F-oo-t-b-a-ll. You wrote football!"

Because verbal prompts can challenge children to broaden their abilities and extend their understanding, knowing when and how to ask appropriate questions is a highly desirable and beneficial skill. Starting a meaningful exchange is a two-step process. First, you must hear and recognize children verbalizing significant thoughts. Then, you respond by rewording their comments into open-ended questions. Continuing to ask questions based on children's responses validates what the child has said and encourages deeper thinking. You want to encourage children to think reflectively and express their thoughts. Ideally, expanded conversations will become written communication.

Upon noticing his construction, Kade's teacher entered the block center and read his journal entry, which prompted the following exchange:

Kade used a set of wooden railway pieces to construct a roller coaster while working in the block center and recorded the experience in his class's Block Journal. His original journal entry is shown below, and the entry he wrote after a conversation with his teacher appears on the next page.

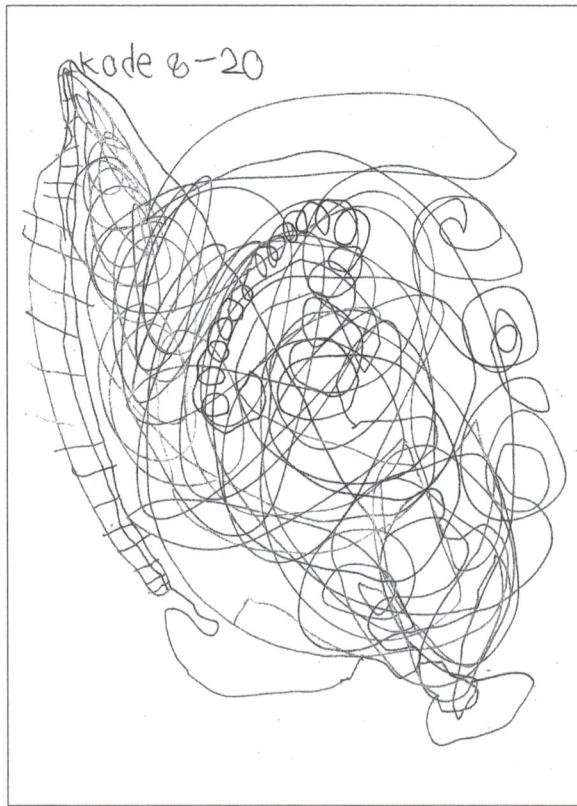

Teacher: *(Pointing to the top of the rollercoaster)* "What's happening here?"

Kade: "That's where it goes up."

Teacher: *(Pointing to an inclined piece of track)* "What's happening here?"

Kade: "It's going down really fast. It's literally going to explode. It's called the Volcano."

Using the open-ended question "What's happening here?" implies that there is meaning behind the child's creation. This same question can be used when pointing to a child's scribble-writing or letter-strings as a means of inviting the child to share his intent. Following their conversation, Kade's teacher encouraged him to expand his original journal entry, and his additional text read "I want to test it. Literally, the name of it is the Volcano."

Kade's journal entry shows the date (August 20) that it was written. There are two useful reasons for dating each entry in a bound collection:
1. to document the frequency of entries; and
2. to chronicle children's growing knowledge of print and writing ability.

Possible Prompt Questions:
"What do you think . . . ?"
"What might happen if . . . ?"
"What happens when . . . ?"
"What else could you do?"
"What is the same/different about . . . ?"
"What materials did you use to . . . ?"
"What tools could you use to . . . ?"
"What steps did you take to . . . ?"
"What do you need to . . . ?"
"What would you do if . . . ?"
"Tell me why . . . ?"
"How do you know . . . ?"
"How could you find out if . . . ?"
"Describe how . . . ?"

These types of questions are more beneficial than asking a direct question such as "What did you make?" because they encourage children's language production and create opportunities to use precise terminology.

A Young Writer's World

Modeling

Encouraging children to talk about their experiences and share their opinions generates topics for conversations and provides the impetus for written communication. Whenever possible, show children what the words used orally look like when written. Educators can display children's thoughts and ideas in print to help them see that a range of views about the same subject is possible.

Additional ways you can encourage children to inform others about their play include: composing messages, leaving notes, or creating signs.

Mrs. Muncaster asked her pre-kindergarteners to expand on their responses to the daily question. She recorded their explanations on chart paper to reinforce the concept that what is said can be written while also demonstrating how print is formed. The completed chart was hung in the classroom to serve as a model for print.

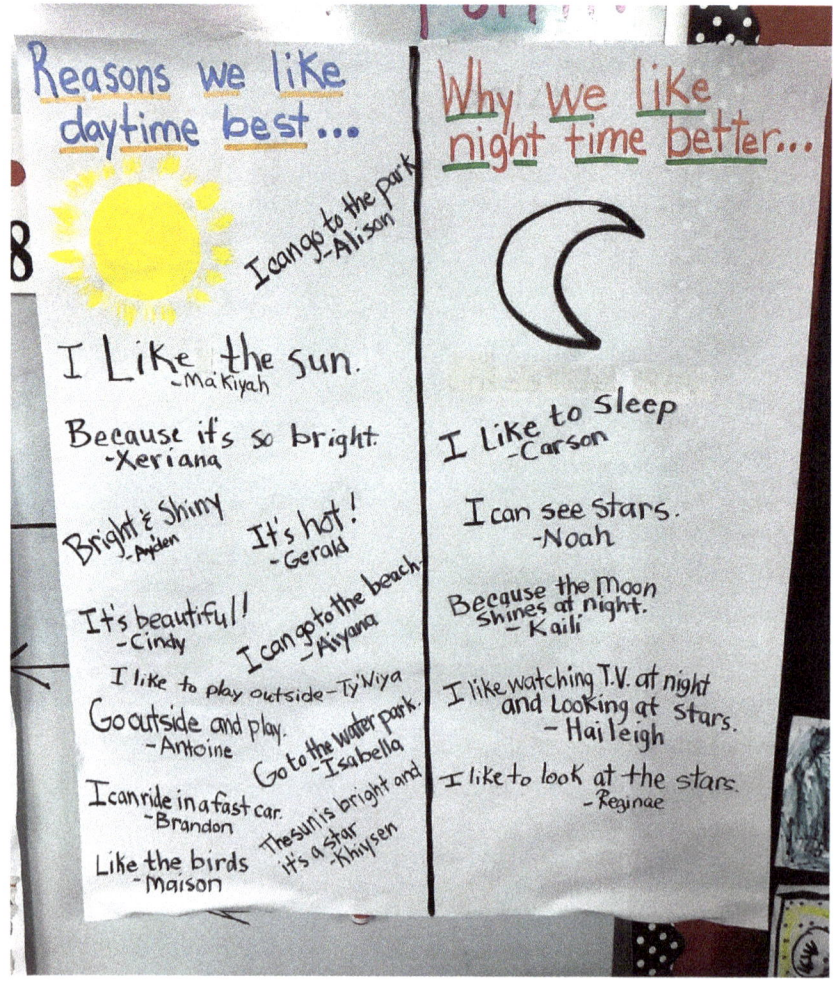

70

When appropriate you can capitalize on and extend children's initial awareness of print's usefulness. For example, promote children's grasp of print as a source of information by helping them find answers to the questions posed during play. Work with the children to search through reference books, websites and other written resources. Then, encourage them to share what they have learned with others.

As children document their play experiences through photographs, pictures, dictation and kid-writing, they demonstrate the purpose of writing in relevant and meaningful ways.

Conclusion

Infusing play with materials that are appropriate, authentic and functional encourages children's writing abilities by providing suitable opportunities to develop new skills and increased understanding. In particular, intentionally selected props for dramatic play and scientific investigations promote literacy behaviors as children actively use many and varied purposes for reading and writing. While literacy objects added to the physical classroom environment can promote literacy behaviors, educators must also consider the role of peer and adult interaction when contemplating ways to promote the expression and exchange of children's ideas in print. Unobtrusive scaffolding of children's writing abilities during meaningful language and literacy contexts embedded within their play can further extend their knowledge of print and encourage children to view themselves as authors.

CHAPTER THREE

Plenty of Print

"One writes to find words' meanings."

-Joy Williams

A Young Writer's World

A wide variety of printed materials in many different forms and styles creates a print-rich environment.

Reading and writing development takes place as children naturally interact with print in their environment. Everything children learn about print through reading benefits them as writers, and different types of text offer unique learning potential. A high-quality writing environment is print-rich. It immerses children in an abundance of materials that provide examples of print, show how print is used, and encourage children's engagement with print. This chapter describes three types of print—books and other resources, environmental print, and purposeful print—and explains ways they each benefit children when you include them in your classroom environment.

Books and Other Print Resources

Children who are learning to read and write need access to meaningful and personally interesting books. Classroom books from all genres of literature and reflecting a wide range of ages, interests, cultures, reading levels, and developmental abilities increase the likelihood that appealing options are available to everyone. Select classic as well as contemporary fiction and nonfiction books to cover an array of topics that span all curricular areas while exposing children to the vast alternatives for illustrating literature. Choosing a variety of trade books, magazines, plays, poetry, newspapers, reference books, picture storybooks, concept books, wordless picture books, predictable books, environmental print books, and picture dictionaries ensures exposure to a diversity of reading options. Through interactions with many types of printed materials, children will expand their language and cognitive skills by learning that written language comes in different forms, has meaning, and meets different purposes.

While the library/listening center is the most obvious place to store books and other reading materials for children to access, it is also beneficial to distribute these throughout the remainder of the classroom.

Incorporating books into every learning center reinforces the understanding that print is everywhere in life.

A Young Writer's World

Display one or more books in each learning center to serve as print models and encourage literacy activities. The simple act of displaying literature nearby may spark children's interest in reading and writing about a particular topic.

You can also include quality children's literature in centers to promote learning across disciplines. This increases children's conceptual understanding along with their knowledge of print.

Art Center

The biography of a famous artist accompanying examples of his work makes an appealing and informative display for the art center that can generate children's interest in reading and writing about a particular medium or artist.

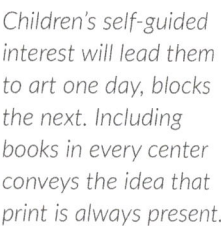

Children's self-guided interest will lead them to art one day, blocks the next. Including books in every center conveys the idea that print is always present.

Plenty of Print

Block Center
Fictional stories and information books in the block center help build vocabulary, inspire creative constructions, and develop literacy skills.

Stories about building and construction are natural inspirations and bring print into the block area.

A Young Writer's World

Publishing Center
Having books about writing and writers in the publishing center increases children's understanding of what it means to be an author.

The publishing center provides an opportunity to create for the purpose of sharing.

With inspiring books and useful materials, children can become absorbed in the process of publishing their own books.

Plenty of Print

After reading and researching different breeds of dogs, Wilder wrote his own informational book for Golden Retrievers. He modeled his cover after a popular classroom series *Blastoff! Readers* and explained how to care for them—

"1. You have to take them to the park.

2. Give them food.

3. Put them in the kennel."

A Young Writer's World

Science Center

Reference and information books are perfect for the science center and can be paired with related fiction to trigger further discussion on topics of study.

Journaling outside might include pressing a leaf, flower or even a bit of dirt onto the page as inspiration for writing.

A reference book on botany inspires children's outdoor observations.

Plenty of Print

To further support developing literacy skills, include books addressing specific print concepts in your learning centers. For example, supply construction-themed alphabet books with wooden letters in the block center or display *A is for Art: An Abstract Alphabet* by Stephen T. Johnson next to the easel in the art center to strengthen children's alphabetic knowledge.

Books that reinforce the theme of each learning center engage children in connecting print and play.

To reinforce the idea of plot by visually representing story sequence through detailed illustrations, consider options such as *How a Book is Made* by Aliki in the publishing center or *How a House is Built* by Gail Gibbons in the block center. Books recommended for each learning center are listed in **Appendix 6 Learning Center Book Lists**.

Environmental Print

Environmental print refers to any text that is naturally occurring within the environment. While environmental print is most commonly associated with words and logos found on product labels, food packages, store signs, and fast-food restaurants, it also includes the temporary print from digital technology, advertising posters, controls on household appliances, stickers, designs on clothing, and graffiti. Exit and restroom signs are examples of typical environmental print in schools. The brand name and model on a computer is another example. Product names, logos, emblems, and sayings on children's shoes, backpacks, and lunchboxes also constitute the type of environmental print often found in classrooms.

All children—regardless of race, socioeconomic status, or home language—encounter environmental print. Although these encounters may vary in amount and type, they are influential because they result from concrete and personal experiences. Since children's ability to read specific environmental print is a result of their repeated exposure to it, the environmental print that children can read varies among individuals and is influenced by both culture and geographic location.

A box of jambalaya mix on a grocery list for the class store might be a commonly recognized example of environmental print in New Orleans but not appropriate in Maine.

Young children who are not yet readers use the significant features and visual cues in environmental print to decode it rather than relying on letter-sound analysis. This process, known as logographic reading, enables non-readers to recognize a limited vocabulary of whole words through incidental cues such as a picture, color, or shape. A printed word is remembered for its unique appearance without associating sounds with symbols. Examples might be the letters and words recognized in logos for stores and products such as Chick-fil-A®, Walmart®, Coca-Cola®, or Cheerios®.

Plenty of Print

Children's ability to read environmental print builds their confidence as readers and allows them to make personal connections to print. Early encounters with environmental print introduce the idea of making sense of symbols and help establish their relationship with reading and writing. When adults draw young children's attention to environmental print, they can increase their awareness of letters, words, and sounds of letters. Children's initial dependence upon graphic features and logos to recognize words gradually decreases as their understanding of letters and print increases. Over time, they begin to apply knowledge learned from reading environmental print to new situations. For example, when 4-year-old Charles first saw his teacher's name in print, he exclaimed, "Hey, Ms. McMillan, you've got three McDonald®'s in your name!"

The presence of environmental print also encourages young children's early attempts at communicating through writing. As children begin to reproduce the words they see around them, environmental print supports their writing by filling one of three distinct functions.

Environmental print contributes to children's writing development by:
1. providing print models,
2. displaying correct spellings of commonly used words, and
3. inspiring writing topics.

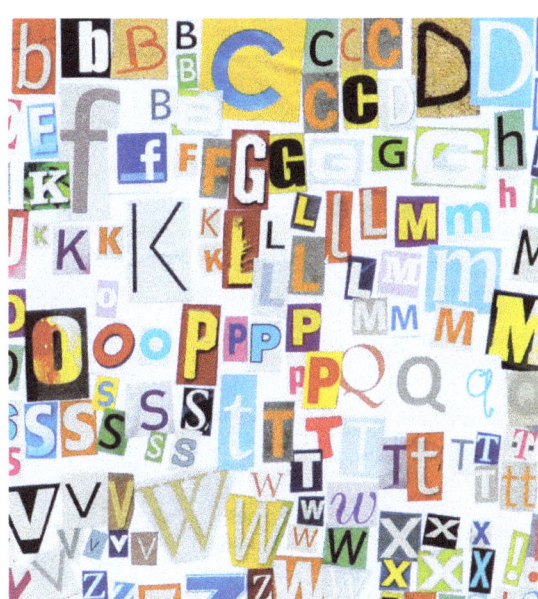

A collage of letters of all shapes and sizes, found in environmental print, helps children see words and letters in the world, outside of books.

Teacher Tip

Use Environmental Print as a Learning Tool
Talk with children about the text found in environmental print. The text that appears in product names and logos usually appears in large, bold capital letters using a variety of sizes, shapes, colors, and fonts. Gradually, children will make the transition from seeing logos as holistic symbols to seeing them as graphics that contain letters and words.

A Young Writer's World

Environmental print can be integrated into learning centers in a variety of ways.

Housekeeping Center

Environmental print on community helper clothing provides an opportunity for reading in the housekeeping center.

Easily recognizable costumes with printed words bring print into pretend play.

84

Plenty of Print

Block Center

Street signs incorporate environmental print into block play while serving as the impetus for stories of a family's driving adventure or a bus driver's record of his cross-county trip.

Playing with real-world traffic signs reinforces the print children see every day on the street.

Library/Listening Center

Environmental print books—both class-made and commercial—enhance the classroom library collection with recognizable print.

Including appropriate newspapers and magazines in the Library Area provides variety for reading and browsing.

Research Highlights

- Early encounters with environmental print, words, and other graphic symbols found in children's surroundings are among their first concrete exposures to written language.[1]
- Children typically read print from their environment before reading print in books.[2]
- Drawing attention to logos and reading them with children encourages the connection between reading and the real world.[3]
- Exposure to environmental print introduces children to making meaning of abstract symbols and offers children their first opportunity to make sense of the world through print.[4]
- Kindergartners' print awareness increased with the use of environmental print materials.[5]

Children begin to enjoy seeing words they know and recognize, all throughout the day.

Plenty of Print

You may also choose to include an assortment of children's literature that depicts environmental print to help children build their written vocabularies and gain knowledge about how print shows up in their daily lives. Books like *I Read Symbols* and *I Read Signs* by Tana Hoban and the *Signs in My World* series by Mary Hill use colorful photographs to show recognizable print in a variety of familiar contexts. Other books, such as *School Bus* by Donald Crews embed environmental print into the illustrations.

Exposure to commonly seen symbols and signs connects children to their larger community.

A Young Writer's World

Purposeful Print

Purposeful print is a type of environmental print that uses a written message to communicate necessary or useful information directly pertaining to the context in which it is found. Examples include posted information related to the current day, special events, or classroom functioning as well as signs, directions, and labels.

Just as adults rely on the signage in an airport or museum to provide important information about their surroundings, children learn from the purposeful print in their classrooms.

Children move the clothespin on this daily schedule to indicate their current activity.

Classroom signs and labels:
1. encourage children's independent interaction with materials,
2. provide print models, and
3. prompt children to use the words displayed when communicating their thoughts and ideas during play.

Visible print labels on objects, bulletin board captions, calendars, notices, announcements, and daily schedules displayed in classrooms demonstrate the practical uses of written language.

Written instructions for classroom procedures, from hand washing to using a tape dispenser to logging onto a computer, provide helpful reminders and authentic reasons for reading.

"Rebus directions," which combine pictures and words to communicate information, assist non-readers in independently accomplishing tasks and are easily made using drawn pictures, clip art, or photographs.

In addition to fostering independence, providing print models, and prompting oral language, written instructions afford the added benefits of:

1. providing practice in following multi-step directions,
2. increasing familiarity with sight words, and
3. displaying correct sentence structure.

You might incorporate signs and labels made by yourself and others written by children and posted as the need arises. With teacher guidance and assistance, even very young children can write informative signs and labels.

Written instructions for classroom procedures provide helpful reminders, authentic reasons for reading, and models of print.

Rebus directions assist children in independently accomplishing tasks while increasing their familiarity with sight words and sentence structure.

Labeling things around the room involves children in organizing and accessing their materials, while providing more exposure to print.

Some signs, such as a reminder to turn off the lights when leaving the classroom, will become permanent classroom fixtures. Others, such as an upcoming field trip announcement, will fill a temporary need and only remain a short time.

A word bank is a very useful type of purposeful print to include in each learning center. A word bank is simply a collection of words to support children's writing. Having a theme-related word bank readily available is a useful tool for expanding children's oral vocabularies as well as extending the use of these words in their written stories and messages. Children incorporate new words into their oral and print vocabularies slowly, after repeated exposure, so the more times they hear and see words, the better. For this reason, many teachers create word walls displaying significant vocabulary, such as high-frequency sight words, children's names, and environmental print that are easily visible throughout the room.

"Spring Words" were displayed in this pre-kindergarten publishing center to encourage their use in verbal and written communication.

Nearly any flat surface can be used for a word wall including bulletin boards, closet doors, cabinet fronts, and the backs or sides of shelves. Including a picture with the words makes the display more effective by increasing children's ability to read and understand the words posted.

Plenty of Print

Evie uses a word wall for support as she writes on the chalkboard.

As discussed in Chapter 2, children's verbal language is enhanced when rich dialogue surrounds their play, and a diverse oral vocabulary positively influences the words children use when writing. Because it is difficult to use rich vocabulary during informal encounters with children without pre-planning, relevant vocabulary and related pictures can be posted on a nearby wall to encourage their use in conversation. Further, having the words clearly displayed in easy view of children provides a model to use when incorporating these words into their own writing.

Another option is a "Word Bank Book" for children to collect new words that they encounter and would like to keep. Word banks written on individual cards that can be easily manipulated is yet another possibility. When used in conjunction with a pocket chart, this type of word bank becomes very interactive.

Environmental Printing

Reading familiar print found in their environment contributes to young children's view of themselves as competent readers and allows them to approach learning to read with increased enthusiasm and confidence. Similarly, copying the print found in their environment contributes to young children's view of themselves as writers because they are able to produce readable text. As their knowledge of print increases, children become aware that "real writing" is composed using a set of predetermined characters known as letters. With this awareness, they begin to supplement their picture and scribble writing with letters and words copied from models found in their surroundings. This is known as environmental printing. Environmental printing is a form of kid-writing that involves copying conventional forms of print directly from sources in their immediate surroundings. Environmental print that is pertinent to children and visible within the context of their ongoing classroom activities supports their writing development in various ways.

Children engage in environmental printing when they use words on display as:

1. a source to copy without regard to its meaning,
2. a resource for the correct spelling of particular words or phrases, and
3. inspiration for a writing topic.

Children's ability to read and/or comprehend the words they are copying is irrelevant as the simple act of copying them evidences their understanding that text is created with letters rather than pictures or symbols. Once children realize that letters and words are needed to write, they begin reproducing surrounding text through environmental printing. Environmental printing allows

Plenty of Print

Wanting to write "first" but not knowing how to form a lower-case "f," Jayden used the alphabet chart in his prekindergarten classroom as a reference.

emerging writers to convey an understandable message to others, and the positive response they receive for this accomplishment reinforces their future attempts at writing the words that they see.

Conclusion

Children who are surrounded by print flourish in literacy development and are often more successful in school. As children observe, read, discuss, and copy the signs and symbols in their world, they become aware that literacy is part of everyone's daily life. Intentionally capitalizing on children's familiarity with environmental print to support early writing attempts is one way to promote progress on their journey to becoming independent authors.

CHAPTER FOUR

Publishing Possibilities

"Writing and rewriting are a constant search for what it is one is saying."

-John Updike

A Young Writer's World

Kai shares writing with his teacher, who listens, asks open-ended questions, and makes supportive observations.

Literacy learning is a social process that occurs in the context of children's interactions with other children and adults. As children develop and practice strategies to communicate through writing, they need to receive feedback. They also need time to reflect on and evaluate their own progress. Equally important, children need others to validate and celebrate their achievements as they take risks, gain new skills, and hone their abilities.

Publishing opportunities affirm children's valuable contributions as writers. Places to publish their work provide a public venue to demonstrate new skills to a receptive audience. The act of publishing celebrates accomplishments along the way to mastery and allows classmates to support each other's efforts through peer response. Publishing their work is also a time when you can show your sincere enthusiasm about children's effort and ability to communicate through print.

Publishing Possibilities

This chapter highlights options for young authors to publish their writing by making it public. These include ideas for using journals and children's literature as catalysts for publishing. It also offers suggestions for displaying children's writing in both traditional and innovative ways.

Published Writing

Within the Introduction of this book, "writing" is defined as encompassing any and all means of written communication including dictation, picture writing, scribbling, and conventional printing. Similarly, a broad interpretation of "publishing" includes any situation where the author conveys a message to someone through writing. Children's "published writing" embodies any writing that is shared with and comprehended by others. The two primary means by which young children compose readable text are dictation and kid writing.

Dictation

Listening to and recording stories as they are told orally introduces children to the purpose of writing and the functions of printed language.[1] Young children's concepts of time and history are limited, so they do not realize the significance of making a record of their stories. Taking dictation facilitates children's awareness of writing's value by increasing their understanding that written records help people remember and share past experiences.

Moriah dictates her story to her teacher, who listens carefully and records every word.

97

A Young Writer's World

Children enjoy the process of dictation as they see their words converted to print.

Dictation is a beneficial tool for increasing children's knowledge of writing. When children observe adults writing the stories they tell, they:
- become aware of the speech-to-text connection,
- gain basic knowledge of sound-symbol relationships, and
- are introduced to the conventions of print.

When children observe others reading their dictated stories, they:
- feel a sense of personal satisfaction,
- witness the power of print, and
- are motivated to write more.

Research Highlights

- Children as young as 2 years old begin to imitate the act of writing by creating drawings and symbolic markings that represent their thoughts and ideas.[2]
- Adults support the emergent writing development of 3- to 5-year-olds by encouraging them to communicate their thoughts and record their ideas using print.[3]
- Young children's ability to write words as they sound has been identified as a direct connection to improved reading scores at the end of first grade.[4]
- Writing has a significant positive impact on an individual's reading ability.[5]

Kid Writing

Children's writing acquisition evolves gradually over time as they progress from making random marks to meaningful symbols. Young children begin by attempting to imitate the writing of others by indiscriminately marking on paper. These early marks evolve into letter-like forms and eventually progress into actual letters. Once children begin to grasp the concept of sound-symbol relationships, their writing becomes much more advanced as letters represent sounds to create a message that is phonetically readable.

While children's initial attempts at written communication have been categorized into different forms of writing[6], they can be collectively referred to as "kid writing" to acknowledge their difference from adult writing.

Children's attempts to communicate using symbols demonstrates their developing awareness of writing. This awareness becomes more refined with increased experience.

Benefits of children's use of early, experimental writing include:
- a growing understanding of print,
- increased awareness of print's purposes, and
- knowledge of print conventions, like capitalization.

Cultivating a light-hearted atmosphere encourages children to play with any form of shape-making, drawing and writing.

Responding to children's kid writing with the understanding that it contains a meaningful message helps children view themselves as authors. This can be accomplished by having children "read" what they have written so that it can be converted into conventional print. Converting kid writing to conventional print is accomplished in much the same way as an adult would take dictation. The adult records the child's interpretation of their kid writing.

Types of Kid Writing

Some of the most common forms of kid writing include picture writing, scribble writing, letter-like forms, letter strings, invented spelling, and conventional spelling. Examples of these forms are shown in the following collection of writing samples, completed by Kindergarten children (pages 100-103).

These writing forms are not sequential stages. Children will use different forms depending on the context of and purpose for their writing, and a child's writing sample may contain more than one form.

Scribble-writing: Scribble-writing is distinctly different from the random scribbles of very young children and often resembles cursive writing. The wavy or looping horizontal marks indicate the child's understanding that writing and drawing are not the same.

Picture-writing: Picture writing occurs when children draw pictures as a means of written communication. Their drawings are intended to tell a story or convey a specific message. Children will often "read" their picture writing with the same tone and intonation used when reading a story aloud.

Letter-like forms: Letter-like forms contain a combination of straight, curved, and intersecting lines resulting in marks that resemble manuscript letters. Letter-like forms, sometimes called mock letters, exhibit children's knowledge of such conventions as left-to-right directionality, spacing and uniformity of size and shape.

Letter strings: Letter strings result when children who have acquired the ability to form some letters and numbers will randomly string the known symbols together to resemble print. Children tend to show preference for letters they know well, like those in their own name. The letters may be formed facing the wrong direction or with slight errors. Letter strings are pre-phonetic, exhibiting no sound-symbol relationship.

Conventional spelling: Conventional spelling results when children have memorized the correct spellings of personally meaningful words, such as names, high frequency words or environmental print.

The example above shows both conventional and invented spelling.

Invented spelling: This term refers to words that are written based on the sounds heard when the word is said and reflects children's knowledge of letters' corresponding sounds. This form is also called kid spelling or sounds-like spelling. At first, children may write a word using a single letter representing only the first or last sound heard. Progressively, children's phonetic writing reaches a point that while not correctly spelled is readable, like "basbol" or "frendz."

An example of appropriate underwriting is shown here. Underwriting is used to increase readability rather than to provide correction.

An adult writing directly below (or above) the child's kid writing is often referred to as "underwriting." Writing the message exactly as it is told preserves the integrity of the message while enabling others to read it. This process makes kid writing readable to others, and having their words read is very motivational for young writers. If questioned, the need for translating a child's message can be explained simply by stating that it helps others to read what the child has written.

Your translation (underwriting) should be viewed as a temporary support as children transition from being able to recognize and form letters to being able to match the corresponding letter to the sounds heard in words. Children who can use "sounds-like" spelling effectively do not need their underwriting because the goal is a readable message, without spelling errors. For this reason, only the parts of the message that cannot be read require underwriting. Several examples are provided in the chart below:

Child's Written Message	Level of Support	Adult Translation
Btrf icadlr fls	Complete	"Butterflies drink nectar from flowers."
I jpt out of the bot	Partial	I jpt out of the bot. jumped boat
i luv u	None	None

Publishing Possibilities

As their phonetic knowledge develops, children will be able to spell more and more words correctly. Correct spelling for commonly used words, such as "the" and "and," along with those that have special meaning for them, like their own names and those of family members, emerge following repeated exposure.

Preserving Speech

A means of recording children's speech is an invaluable tool for capturing children's oral language. Insightful comments and astute remarks made during whole group discussions can be preserved and transcribed later. Recording children's oral stories allows them to share their ideas regardless of print knowledge, fine-motor skills, or handwriting abilities. When replayed later, the oral accounts serve as an assessment of children's knowledge of story structure or show progress in vocabulary and sentence development. Once transcribed, they become readable text that is personally meaningful.

Teacher Tip

Use Turtle Talk
To assist children using invented spelling, model how to stretch out a word saying it slowly as each individual sound is emphasized. Encourage children to listen for and represent every sound on paper as it is heard.

A student sounds out the parts of a word as her teacher repeats it slowly, one syllable at a time.

105

A Young Writer's world

Teacher Tip

Activate Classroom Communication
A message station or class mailbox system encourages and organizes written communication between teachers and children or between children themselves. A daily report or weekly newsletter written or dictated by children facilitates communication between school and home.

Classroom Chronicles

Young children are primarily interested in writing as a means of sharing their ideas. As a result, young children's writing abilities are best developed and published through genuine experiences as authors. Making a class diary, scrapbook, or captioned photo album is a compelling place to begin. Whether their contributions are dictated or written, the experience of communicating in print furthers their writing development while providing a detailed, chronological record of classroom events that may be otherwise forgotten.

Journals

Recording individual experiences in a journal format appeals to children's egocentric nature and provides a sequential view of their writing development. There are many advantages to journaling.

Keeping a journal:
- improves writing fluency,
- provides practice for mechanics of writing,
- helps children reflect on ideas,
- provides a real-life purpose for writing,
- builds confidence in writing abilities.

A journal is a special place for a child to collect their own drawings, words, and explorations.

Types of Journals for Early Childhood Classrooms

Personal journals primarily for recording daily events, thoughts, and reflections.

Dialogue journals are a written conversation resulting when teachers respond to children's journal entries.

Field journals are for children to document their outdoor observations.

Traveling journals allow a stuffed animal serving as class mascot to go home with a different child at the end of each day along with a journal for recording his nightly adventures. The previous entry, recorded by parent or other family member as told by the child, is read before the teacher selects the next child.

Book review journal and single book from a favorite storybook series, like *Clifford the Big Red Dog* or *Curious George*, is periodically sent home with a different child. After reading the book at home, children write a book review with parents serving as scribe or providing the underwriting, to be shared with classmates.

Family message journal is for children to write about books, school activities, and other experiences to be shared with family members who in turn respond.

A Young Writer's World

Giving children an opportunity to keep a daily journal has become an established practice in many early childhood classrooms.

Children record special times and daily experiences, seeing the stories in their own life.

Share Writing with Families
When possible, broaden children's understanding and mastery of writing skills and composition strategies by enlisting families' interest, appreciation, and support of journal writing.

Kindergarten children and their families recorded Silent Sammy's adventures in this traveling journal.

Literature-Inspired Publishing Possibilities

As children hear, read and discuss stories from books, they begin to freely adopt their favorite parts into the stories they tell. Encourage your students to deliberately incorporate and intermingle familiar characters, settings or events as a way to transition into writing and publishing their own original stories.

Retellings, Rewrites and Innovations on Texts

Children's first encounters writing narrative text can occur in the form of retellings. Children, either individually or working collaboratively with peers, can create a personalized version of a familiar story retold in their own words. Similarly, children can rewrite a favorite tale by altering one or more elements. By changing the point of view, character or setting, children produce a unique story within a familiar framework. Examples of rewrites include *The True Story of the Three Little Pigs*, *The Gingerbread Girl*, and *Cindy Ellen: A Wild West Cinderella*.

Friends can partner to rewrite a favorite story, with new twists and turns.

Using a recognizable structure from a well-known story or song is another option for writing original narrative accounts in a supportive context. These stories, known as innovations on texts, allow inexperienced writers to imitate the masters on their way to becoming accomplished authors themselves. The repetitive and predictable text of *It Looked Like Spilt Milk* by Charles Shaw or the series of *There Was an Old Lady Who Swallowed* books by Lucille Colandro both offer easy and fun formats that can be adapted for class books. For example, one prekindergarten class wrote a Halloween tale called *Little Pumpkin, Little Pumpkin, What Do You See?* using the engaging structure from Bill Martin's classic *Brown Bear, Brown Bear, What Do You See?*

Six-year-old Tucker used Hey, Little Ant by Phillip M. Hoose, Hannah Hoose, and Debbie Tilley as a model text for his original narrative.

Model Texts

Using model or mentor text to facilitate children's writing development, teaches children to emulate the author's craft and begin writing like the authors whose books they love. Various books can be used to help children examine writing conventions such as dialogue, figurative language and repetition for the purpose of incorporating such elements into their own stories.

Suitable model texts are:
- pleasingly simple,
- contain interesting language and
- can be read independently by the child.

Publishing in Centers

Giving authors the option to share their published work with their classmates brings fun and connection.

Motivation and chance of success increase with opportunities for collaboration, and learning centers are naturally social settings. Learning centers create a pleasurable, supportive environment in which mistakes are inconsequential and which, as a result, can serve a significant role in supporting writing development. In an accepting atmosphere, children communicate using various forms of kid writing while adults and peers serve as tutors and collaborators.

By focusing on the materials provided, along with their placement within the classroom, you can significantly increase children's opportunities to publish.

Publishing Possibilities

While library book check-out slips, waiting lists for popular activities, and daily sign-in as attendance provide functional writing opportunities, they seldom go beyond requiring the child to write his name. Expressive writing, however, helps children acquire and develop writing skills while also increasing general knowledge. If children are to acquire and develop their writing skills, writing in centers must move beyond being functional to include numerous opportunities for participation in expressive writing activities in a wide range of situations for multiple purposes. Functional and Expressive writing are compared in the chart below:

Invite children to describe anything they see or enjoy in the classroom environment.

Center	Functional Writing	Expressive Writing
Blocks	Waiting list	Journal entry
Computer	Sign-in sheet	Evaluating a website in the computer center directory
Housekeeping	Shopping list	Instructions for babysitter
Library	Book check-out slip	Review of book read
Science	Checklist for activities completed	Recording observations of the class pet

Writing in learning centers should be
- expressive in nature,
- occur in a wide range of situations, and
- meet multiple purposes.

A Young Writer's World

To increase opportunities for expressive writing, each learning center must have opportunities for publishing. That is to say that every center must provide a way for children to share their learning experiences with adults and peers through writing. Some specific examples are provided on the following pages.

Specific labeling on children's artwork gives a sense of pride in publishing and helps classmates experience each other's work.

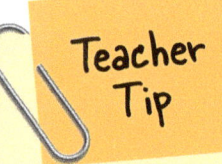

Write-and-Share Center Stories
Allow a few minutes immediately before clean-up for writing. Then, allow children to report on their center accomplishments during whole group using their pictures, dictation, or stories to accompany the oral account of what they did.

Publishing in the Art Center
Museum Placards
Opportunities to expand writing abilities and artistic knowledge occur when children are encouraged to make museum placards to accompany their displayed art. Typically, these small signs include the title of the work, followed by the date and place of creation, and the materials or technique used. These informative labels provide a perfect opportunity for publishing that incorporates art-specific vocabulary and makes classroom displays more meaningful to viewers.

Publishing Possibilities

Portfolios

Unlike wall displays, a portfolio offers a portable showcase of a child's artwork. Folding a piece of poster board in half and securing the short edges with staples or wide tape makes a large, flat case for storing and transporting drawings, paintings, collages, printmaking, or other two-dimensional art projects. Children publish as they create written products, such as a description of their subject, list of materials used, or outline of the steps taken, to accompany their artwork. The writing can be done directly on the artwork, on the back of the picture, or on a separate piece of paper that is attached to the art.

Children enjoy having a portfolio as a special place to collect their work.

Publishing in the Block Center

Digital Stories

An inexpensive digital camera and means of printing the pictures provides an enticing way for children to capture their block play. Creating captions to accompany their pictures provides a publishing opportunity that challenges children's thinking and skill as authors. Digital photos are particularly useful for generating the following types of writing related to building:

- Before and after
- Sequence of events
- Series of steps
- Cause and effect

Photos make a wonderful addition to children's journals, capturing impermanent creations like block structures and sculptures.

When these written products are sent home and shared with families who rarely have the chance to admire block center accomplishments that occur at school, children's status as author is further affirmed.

A Young Writer's World

Child-Authored Block Books

When children contribute to class-made books, they better understand the role of authors and illustrators. Further, they feel a sense of ownership and pride that increases relevance and makes these books immediate favorites for repeated reading.

Options for the block center library include:

1. **Rewriting a Familiar Favorite**

   Children's vocabulary and creativity are challenged as they work collaboratively to compose and illustrate original versions of a building-themed book such as *A House is a House for Me* by Mary Ann Hoberman. The finished product is sure to inspire the building of some unique homes.

2. **Make a Book of World Structures**

   Involve children in searching for photos on the Internet (make sure to choose those that are permitted for personal/classroom use), in travel magazines or from old calendars showing such famous buildings as Big Ben, the Eiffel Tower, Blue Mosque, Great Wall of China, Taj Mahal, Stonehenge, Parthenon, Sydney Opera House, and Leaning Tower of Pisa. Mount and label each picture with its name and location. Then, laminate and bind pages together or place inside page protectors in a 3-ring notebook. This inspirational book will stimulate an abundance of building along with opportunities to talk and write about different people and places.

Visual representations of famous buildings in the world add beauty and interest while inspiring children's block or art creations.

A whiteboard in the math center gives children a chance to "teach" one another as they learn.

Publishing in the Math Center
Three Column Charts
Mathematical explorations provide young children with opportunities to record all kinds of observations. Posting a large, 3-column chart in the math center creates space for children to publish their discoveries along with their queries. These charts allow children to share their knowledge with others and shape the learning process by posing questions others may be challenged to answer. Two charts to try: "I Know, I Want to Know, I Learned" and "I Think, I Notice, I Wonder."

Creating Counting Books
Counting books vary. There are endless possibilities for constructing and illustrating counting books. They can be any shape, size or design. Illustrations can be drawn, painted, computer-generated, or collage. Begin by exposing children to a variety of counting books. Books like *On the Launch Pad: A Counting Book About Rockets* by Michael Dahl, *Fish Eyes: A Book You Can Count On* by Lois Ehlert or *Ten Black Dots* by Donald Crews, that can be used as model texts.

A Young Writer's World

Teacher Tip

Celebrate Math Stories
Recognized on September 25, National Math Storytelling Day encourages everyone to tell stories through math. Help students connect literacy and numeracy using a popular math story book (see *Appendix 6: Learning Center Book Lists* for suggestions) as your read aloud and assist children in realizing that stories have numbers in them and that they can publish their own!

The text for counting books can take several different forms. Several examples are provided below:
- Pictorial representations: 🍎🍎🍎🍎🍎
- Numeric representations: 5, 4+1, 3+2, 6-1, 0+5, 10-5
- Poetry: Five bees in a hive.
- Related lists: high fives, five fingers, five toes
- Riddles: I am less than 8. I am more than 2. I sound like drive.

Publishing is essential for supporting and sustaining emerging writers. Repeated and varied publishing experiences encourage and enable emerging writers by creating a perception of themselves as authors while providing immediate recognition and affirmation of their effort.

Finding and celebrating counting in storybooks adds another activity and connection in the math center.

Portable Publishing

The possibilities for publishing become boundless when portable writing centers are added. A portable writing center is a small collection of items to write on and with, that can be easily transported for use in a variety of locations.

Portable Publishing
- increases classroom center choices,
- establishes opportunities for writing outdoors, and
- makes rest time more meaningful for children who are not sleeping.

Providing writing materials in a movable container instantly makes writing an appealing endeavor that can be accomplished anytime anywhere.

A portable publishing center encourages children to get up and go with their writing, bringing it along, anywhere they want to explore.

Possible Containers for Portable Publishing		
storage box	beach bag	small cooler
tackle box	purse	picnic basket
tool box	gift bag	small suitcase
briefcase	canvas tote	make-up bag
backpack	lunch box	apron (tool or cooking)

A Young Writer's World

Children take pride in seeing their work displayed around the classroom.

Writing Displays

As children attempt new roles as writers, positive response is paramount for continued improvement. The feedback received needs to be consistently supportive and instructive.

Displaying children's pictures, attempts at writing, or dictated stories affirms children's status as users and creators of print by making them published authors.

Prominently displaying written explanations of children's work reflects the amount of time and effort they expended to build a skyscraper using unit blocks or paint their family using watercolors. Wall space is not required for displaying children's work. See "Ideas for Displaying Children's Work" for some suggested alternatives.

Publishing Possibilities

When children choose and display their own writing, it is sure to appear at the child's eye-level, and frees adults from what can become a cumbersome task of continually updating items on display.

Giving children ownership of display space also increases their pride in and responsibility for the room's appearance while producing a child-centered atmosphere not present when commercial decorations or teacher-created exhibits dominate the classroom. As with the writing itself, perfection in the display is not expected. The amateurish displays that children create confirm your value of their efforts and sincere contributions, over the need for precision and absolute accuracy.

Individual display space allows children to publish self-selected writing that can be rotated without adult assistance.

Ideas for Displaying Children's Work

- string a clothesline
- suspend individual clothespins or plastic clips from the ceiling using clear fishing line
- attach papers to window blinds with paperclips
- outline space on cabinet doors, restroom walls, or along the hallway to make mini bulletin boards
- transform the side of a filing cabinet into a magnetic display space
- provide individual display spaces for each child throughout the room

Publishing Beyond the Classroom

Displaying children's writing is only one of many options available for publishing their stories. A key part of keeping publishing an encouraging and motivational moment is sharing children's writing with an audience beyond the classroom. There are many authentic ways to facilitate writing for an expanded audience whether it be school-wide, world-wide, or somewhere in between.

Letters

By its very nature, letter-writing provides the opportunity to address a real and specific audience. Whether delivered electronically or in an envelope, writing and sending a letter may clearly illustrate the purpose of writing as written communication better than any other form of writing. Letter writing also provides the ideal setting for exposing children to the different types of writing, since they can be written to entertain, persuade or inform.

Letter writing lets children share and direct their writing to the world beyond the classroom.

Children's literature can provide both examples of and the impetus for letter writing. Enjoyable and educational models for corresponding in print can be found in a variety of books including Mark Teague's *Dear Mrs. LaRue: Letters from Obedience School* or *Dear Mr. Blueberry* by Simon James. The author-illustrator team of Pat Brisson and Rick Brown introduce readers to the likeable, travel-bound Kate in a series of picture books that chronicle her adventures, through letters home. Composing a letter to a favorite children's author and/or illustrator allows children to use writing to discuss writing.

In addition to letters, thank you notes, invitations, postcards, and "get well" messages offer a genuine purpose for writing that is sure to be read and that might even generate a written response.

School and Community
Individual pieces of writing can be selected for publication in a lightweight, inexpensive frame or on poster board and displayed prominently in the office area, on cafeteria walls, or along hallways. Similar displays at a local bookstore or branch of the public library allow family and community members to acknowledge children's writing efforts in a highly visible arena.

Online Resources
Children's work can be published in a school newsletter or webpage, and a range of websites specialize in publishing various forms of children's writing, from stories and poems to jokes and book reviews.

Conclusion

Taking dictation and underwriting are recommended practices in publishing children's initial attempts at communicating through print. Allowing children to make their writing available for others to read and enjoy serves as strong motivation for continued writing. There are many ways to share children's writing as part of the normal day-to-day routine and with an audience beyond the classroom.

CHAPTER FIVE

Writing Role Models

"Our admiration of fine writing will always be in proportion to its real difficulty and its apparent ease."

-Charles Caleb Colton

While beneficial, simply providing writing materials and presenting opportunities to publish are in and of themselves not enough. As you demonstrate how these materials are used, model the act of writing and provide guidance in writing activities where children could not be successful on their own, children grow as authors. Daily exposure to writing models helps children build knowledge about writing and piques their curiosity about an activity generally perceived as grown-up. This chapter discusses young children's need for adult writers in their environment.

Writing Role Models

Children's ability to write evolves gradually over time as they experiment with the process of putting random marks, and later, meaningful symbols, down on paper. Their expanding knowledge of writing increases every time they observe a competent writer. Adult writers demonstrate when, why, and how writing is used. Through their observation of writers writing, children receive powerful lessons in the fundamentals of communicating through print.

As children consistently witness others engaged in the act of writing, they begin to internalize the following concepts:

- Writing occurs from left to right and from top to bottom.
- Written words convey a message.
- Space is needed between letters in a word and words in a sentence.
- Punctuation marks are used along with letters and words to communicate meaning.
- There is a predictable correspondence between the sounds heard in words and the letters used to represent them.
- Each letter has a correct formation.

Writing Role Models

A role model is a person who inspires and encourages others to reach their fullest potential. With support and guidance from writing role models, young children become authors, composing their own stories that they eagerly share with others.

Parents as Partners

Children learn to write much the same way that they learn to walk and talk—by observing and copying others. When learning to write, however, children have the added benefit of being able to use oral language. As they learn to write, they listen to and ask questions of those they are trying to imitate.

Most young children are fascinated with the process of writing and begin putting marks on paper at an early age. Children flourish in a home environment that encourages their experimentation with writing through access to writing materials and family members who serve as writing models, scribes, and enthusiastic supporters.

Teachers and family members inspire children by sharing their own enjoyment in the writing process.

As discussed in Chapter 2, the amount and variety of writing materials made available influences how writing is integrated into children's play. Children playing house are more likely to take a phone message if self-adhesive notes and a pen are sitting nearby. For this reason, children need access to a variety of writing tools and supplies when playing. Items similar to those found in the classroom—pencils, pens, crayons, markers, paper, and note pads—should also be available for their use at home. Similarly, handing a 5-year-old a pad and pencil while preparing a meal can be the impetus for her writing down what each family member would like to drink. These types of play experiences in which children mimic the behavior of adults offer meaningful experiences with print.

Every list made, at home or at school, is an opportunity to share writing with children.

Children are keen observers of their parents' behavior because this is where they get the information for how to behave like an adult. There are many opportunities for parents to serve as writing role models. As parents jot down a note, make a grocery list, write a check, or address an envelope, they are modeling why and how to write. Parents can capitalize on these informal learning opportunities by talking about what they are writing as they do it. For example, while making a list of errands, they can say out loud what is being written. "First, we will go to the bank, next the cleaners, and then the grocery store."

In addition to the valuable information gained through watching others write, children who cannot yet write independently benefit from having a parent or older sibling serve as a scribe. As discussed in Chapter 4, children begin to recognize the need for putting words on paper when others take dictation and read their words back to them. Children rely on the adults in their environment to help them understand that print is speech written down and that writing allows us to share our words at a later time or with people not initially present.

At-Home Writing Opportunities:
- names of guests for birthday party
- ingredients needed for a favorite recipe
- a letter to someone deployed in military
- a thank you note
- a story to share with a relative who lives far away.

Writing opportunities, along with encouraging words, give children the feeling of being competent writers. Just like learning other tasks, such as feeding themselves or riding a bike, children learn to write through trial-and-error, and the process can be both messy and frustrating. Experimentation is an important part of learning to write, and much practice is required. Positive words from caring adults provide the motivation to keep trying.

Genuine encouragement and attention to details validates children's efforts and inspires them to continue.

Teachers as Writing Models

While writing is a part of almost everything teachers do throughout the day, it is often a quiet, solitary pursuit, and you must make a conscious effort to call children's attention to your use of writing. There are many authentic opportunities to model writing throughout the day as a part of both whole group activities and individual interactions.

Opportunities for whole group modeling are most likely to occur during circle time as part of the daily routine or a lesson. One popular example of teachers serving as writing models is the morning message. The morning message is a time for children to think about what is going to be happening during the school day, to reflect on an event that occurred before, or to discuss a meaningful upcoming event. You may choose to make the morning message open-ended or predictable. An example of writing the morning message using a consistent pattern each day is shown below:

Good Morning,
Today is Friday. Our leader is Juan. He likes to play basketball.

The day, leader's name, and favorite activity or food changes daily while the basic structure remains the same. Using a recognizable pattern, assists children in reading the message. The repetition allows children to become familiar with high frequency sight words while the variation keeps the message interesting and provides exposure to new words and letter sounds.

The daily news is similar to the morning message in composition and purpose, but written at the end of the day. Composed prior to dismissal, it provides information about the day's events. The content for the daily news can be generated by an individual child or several children who comment on something that occurred during the day. At the beginning of the year, a short, two or three line message is sufficient. The content and length of these daily messages, however, will change as the year and children's abilities progress.

This morning message is an example of a cloze activity, where children contribute text by filling in the blanks.

Writing Role Models

Children enjoy and learn from the ritual of watching and hearing their teacher speak the morning message aloud, while simultaneously writing it on the board.

More advanced messages that do not follow a predictable pattern may be used later in the year. The morning message example below offers a way to introduce additional punctuation marks (comma and exclamation point), numerals incorporated into text, and new print conventions (underlining book titles).

It is Monday, April 10, 2017. Today we are going to read The Tiny Seed by Eric Carle. After reading, we will plant our own seeds!

Another option is to convert the morning message into a cloze activity. This is done by inserting little blank lines in the message to indicate spaces for children to fill-in letters or words that they know.

The most important aspect of a daily message is that children see it being written. Regardless of format, the message is created in the children's presence as opposed to being written in advance. In order to maximize the learning potential, children need the experience of seeing spoken words recorded on paper. A pre-written message from teachers to children can serve as text for shared reading but does not provide the opportunity for

Teacher Tip

Make the Most of Messages
Provide further interaction with the morning message throughout the day by:
- providing a pointer for children to track print while reading,
- cutting it apart to be used as a puzzle in a pocket chart or on the floor,
- binding each month's worth of messages into books for the class library.

129

A Young Writer's World

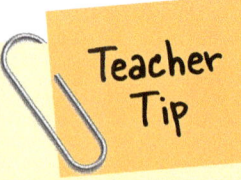

Teacher Tip

Remember these Modeling Musts
1. The child or children should be able to see you as you are writing.
2. Say the words as you write them, talking the children through your process of writing the message.
3. Show enthusiasm for and enjoyment of writing while you demonstrate the mechanics of writing.

children to observe print being created. You model the writing process when you write the messages, with children watching as you say each word as you write it, and note particular practices like, "I'm starting with the letter E because that is the first letter in Eric's name." This interactive process, which is both engaging and motivational, eventually leads to the point where children begin to incorporate the concepts, letters, and words modeled into their own writing.

Teachers often model writing to individual children as they work in centers or during journal writing as occasions naturally arise. A planned occurrence for individual modeling can take place daily using "Happy Notes." Identify one to three children each day as the recipient of a special note home, acknowledging a kind deed, or sharing a noteworthy accomplishment. Prior to dismissal, the teacher invites each selected child to privately watch as she composes their personal note while verbalizing each word written. In addition to being a form of positive communication between school and home, this practice reinforces the function of writing as a means of communicating with those who are not present while showing the child how print is created.

When children see their teachers writing, they receive a powerful message that writing is both useful and valued. As writing is both observed and practiced as a part of the normal classroom routine, children acquire knowledge of writing along with a desire to use that knowledge voluntarily and often.

Teachers encourage young children's writing development when they:

- Model writing for different purposes throughout the classroom to both groups and individuals.

- Take dictation frequently as a means of connecting spoken and written words for children.

Writing Role Models

- Think out loud about print conventions when modeling writing to provide additional information about the writing process. Such as, explaining the use of quotation marks to indicate that someone is speaking.

- Are available during center time to observe, replenish supplies, and help when needed, to demonstrate the integration of writing in children's play.

- Make casual, incidental teaching points about letter formation and/or sound-symbol correspondence while modeling.

Teachers encourage children's writing by witnessing their process, listening to their ideas, and offering enthusiastic support.

Research Highlights

- Many prospective teachers hold a negative view of themselves as writers and, often, a dislike of writing, reporting that they are unsure of how to teach writing and unaware of the benefits that writing contributes to lifelong learning.[1]
- Teachers' conceptions of literacy and their own literate identities, frame, shape, and often limit students' identities as writers.[2]
- A teacher's self-perception as a writer affects classroom practices.[3]

Teachers as Authors

Along with being writing role models, the best writing teachers are also authors. Your own personal writing experiences help you better assist children who struggle to get the right words down on paper. Being a writer yourself also helps you retain your vulnerability as a learner and sensitivity to the complex challenges of putting thoughts into written words.

As a proficient writer, you know that it is less difficult and more fulfilling to complete self-selected writing tasks, like a long letter to a dear friend, as opposed to those that are assigned, like a yearly report. This is also true for children learning to write, who need opportunities to choose their own writing topics and projects, which will be easier to sustain and more gratifying.

Teachers can draw upon their own joys and challenges with the writing process, to relate to young writers and encourage their experimentation and perseverance.

Drawing upon your own experience as an author, it is easy to see that accomplished writers are in control of their own writing. They determine its purpose, pace, and even the method itself. Young children on the road to becoming accomplished authors need to be given this same responsibility by being allowed to make decisions regarding their writing. In addition, they need opportunities to examine and hone the craft of writing—an endeavor equally important to those who teach writing.

Teachers' encounters as writers provide firsthand experience needed to effectively guide their interactions with young writers. If you are not a confident writer yourself, you may not feel adequately equipped to teach writing. Children best benefit from an understanding of writing that has intrinsic value to them.

In order to provide meaningful writing experiences for your students, you, ideally, have experienced the power and satisfaction of writing as a means of learning and self-expression. If not, you might be unaware of how challenging and rewarding the act of writing as an author can be.

Why write?
When teachers write, they:

1. Provide a positive model for children.
2. Show that writing is valuable, purposeful, and enjoyable.
3. Demystify the act of writing for children.
4. Remove the image of author as an anonymous, obscure individual.
5. Can empathize with children's writing struggles.

Conclusion

Learning to write is a very long journey that begins early in childhood. Before children can begin to string letters together to make words, they have much to learn. This learning begins to emerge in their homes and early childhood classrooms as they imitate the writing behaviors displayed in their surroundings. Most children learn about writing through playing at writing. They need the tools and materials of writers as well as the gentle guidance of supportive role models to learn the usefulness of writing.

Family members and teachers play an important role in promoting young children's writing development. Children flourish as writers when experiences with writing are present at home as well as at school. Adults who provide materials and opportunities for writing, serve as role models and scribes, and offer supportive encouragement become partners in the process of young children's transition to becoming authors who write with purpose and joy.

APPENDICES

Appendix 1A is available in a digital format for easy printing at:
ExchangePress.com/writer

APPENDIX 1A
Record of Learning Center Use by Class

Date: _____

Children's Names																				
Art																				
Block																				
Computer																				
Fine Motor																				
Housekeeping																				
Library/ Listening																				
Math																				
Publishing																				
Science																				

Appendix 1B is available in a digital format for easy printing at:
ExchangePress.com/writer

APPENDIX 1B
Monthly Record of Child's Learning Center Participation

Child's Name: _____

Date																				
Day of the week	Monday	Tuesday	Wednesday	Thursday	Friday	Monday	Tuesday	Wednesday	Thursday	Friday	Monday	Tuesday	Wednesday	Thursday	Friday	Monday	Tuesday	Wednesday	Thursday	Friday
Art																				
Block																				
Computer																				
Fine Motor																				
Housekeeping																				
Library/Listening																				
Math																				
Publishing																				
Science																				

APPENDIX 2
Center Materials

	Art	Blocks	Computer	Fine Motor	Housekeeping	Libarary/Listening	Math	Publishing	Science
Children's literature and magazines	X	X	X	X	X	X	X	X	X
Teacher, child, and class-made books	X	X	X	X	X	X	X	X	X
Environmental print (i.e., on packages)	X	X	X	X	X	X	X	X	X
Authentic print (i.e., signs, labels, directions)	X	X	X	X	X	X	X	X	X
Letter/number sets (i.e., foam, blocks, pasta, tiles, beads)				X			X	X	
Sensory letters/numbers (i.e., sandpaper, felt, fur, foil)				X			X	X	
Magnetic letters/numbers/shapes and trays				X			X	X	
Letter/number puzzles				X			X	X	
Letter/number matching or memory cards				X			X	X	
Letter/number sponges	X			X			X	X	
Letter/number stickers	X			X			X	X	
Letter/number stamps and ink pad	X			X			X	X	
Letter/number/shape stencils and templates	X			X			X	X	
Letter/number path or stepping stones								X	
Upper and lower case matching cards								X	
Number and number word matching cards							X	X	
Letter and beginning/ending sound picture cards								X	
Number line							X		
100s Number chart							X		
Rulers, yardsticks, and tape measures	X	X					X	X	X
Alphabet chart								X	
Counters (i.e., buttons, beads, cubes, straws) and tubs							X		X

Appendices

Print-related materials appear in italics. **Publishing/bookmaking materials appear in bold.**	Art	Blocks	Computer	Fine Motor	Housekeeping	Libarary/Listening	Math	Publishing	Science
Pocket chart and word cards	X	X	X	X	X	X	X	X	X
Dominoes, dice, number cubes, and spinners							X		X
Abacas							X		X
Calculator					X		X		X
Number games (i.e., Bingo, Go Fish, Yahtzee, Uno)				X			X		X
Language games (i.e., lotto, Scrabble, Boggle, Letter Bingo)				X			X	X	X
Graph paper (½ and 1 inch) and blank bar graphs		X					X	X	X
Index cards and sentence strips	X	X	X	X	X	X	X	X	X
Self-adhesive notepads and labels of various sizes	X	X						X	X
Adding machine tape and blank number lines							X	X	
Chalk/chalkboard or dry erase board/markers			X				X	X	
Stapler and staples	X							X	
Hole puncher and 3-ring hole puncher	X			X				X	
Yarn, string, ribbon, twine, and cloth	X							X	
Construction paper in various colors/sizes	X							X	
Drawing paper and newsprint in various sizes	X							X	X
Masking and scotch tape	X							X	
Paste, glue, and glue sticks	X							X	
Blank books of various shapes/sizes	X	X	X	X	X	X	X	X	X
Tempera Paint, different size brushes, and easel	X			X					
Finger paint and finger paint paper	X			X					
Mural paper	X	X			X			X	X

141

APPENDIX 2
Center Materials
(continued)

	Art	Blocks	Computer	Fine Motor	Housekeeping	Libarary/Listening	Math	Publishing	Science
Picture album of past creations/constructions	X	X							
Word wall	X	X	X	X	X	X	X	X	X
Poems, rhymes, and chants on chart paper	X	X	X	X	X	X	X	X	X
Motivational/Informational posters and quotes	X		X			X	X	X	X
Blocks (i.e., unit, cardboard, foam, hollow, colored)		X		X			X		
Wooden or plastic multicultural people/animals		X			X				X
Vehicles, ramps, and roads		X							
Street signs and road maps		X							
Barn, dollhouse, or other floor toys		X			X				
Career hats, non-stereotyped clothes, and uniforms		X			X				
Purses, suitcases, briefcases, and backpacks					X				
Hoops and wands		X							
Steering wheels and tires		X							
Boxes and packing materials (small and appliance size)	X	X							
Unbreakable mirrors		X			X				X
Blueprints, house plans, and real estate brochures		X							
Clipboard and notepad		X			X				X
Invoices, order forms, envelopes, and receipt books		X			X		X	X	X
Building/User/Observation/Reading log		X	X				X		X
Computer and software			X						
Living books			X						
Puppets, puppet stage, and *scripts*							X		X

Appendices

Print-related materials appear in italics. **Publishing/bookmaking materials appear in bold.**	Art	Blocks	Computer	Fine Motor	Housekeeping	Libarary/Listening	Math	Publishing	Science
Child-sized kitchen set (i.e., sink, stove, refrigerator, table)					X				
Dishes (i.e., pots/pans, silverware, utensils, and bowls)				X	X				
Measuring spoons/cups and graduated cylinders (plastic)				X	X		X		X
Multicultural plastic foods and *food containers*					X				
Phones, phonebook and message pad					X				
Class addresses and phone list					X			X	
TV Guide, newspaper					X				
Department store ads, grocery ads, and coupons					X	X			
Cookbook and recipe cards					X				X
Compass, maps, globe, and atlases					X	X			X
Seasonal items (i.e., leaves, seeds, icicles)									X
Nature collections (i.e., seashells, rocks, seeds, insects)									X
Class pet(s) (i.e., ant farm, aquarium, hamster, tadpoles)									X
Prisms and kaleidoscopes	X								X
Indoor/outdoor thermometer and rain gauge							X		X
Magnifiers, microscopes, and binoculars				X					X
Tweezers and plastic droppers				X					X
Balance/Bathroom scale and weights							X		X
Marbles/balls and plastic piping		X		X					X
Potted plants and sprouts									X
Bones, dental molds, and x-rays									X
Growth (height and weight) charts							X		X

143

APPENDIX 2
Center Materials
(continued)

	Art	Blocks	Computer	Fine Motor	Housekeeping	Libarary/Listening	Math	Publishing	Science
Rain/weather charts and graphs							X		X
Data collection and observation record sheets/charts	X	X	X			X	X	X	X
Calendars (daily, weekly, monthly, and yearly)							X		X
Puzzles and tangrams				X	X		X		
Stacking cups and nesting blocks	X				X				
Construction toys (i.e., Legos, K'Nex, Tinker Toys)		X			X				
Beads and laces					X		X		
Lacing cards					X				
Dressing dolls or boards					X				X
Pattern blocks, Unifix cubes, and attribute blocks					X		X		
Peg boards and pegs of different sizes					X		X		
Geoboards and rubber bands					X		X		
Tracing cards (letters, numbers, and words)				X			X	X	
Playdough/clay and accessories	X				X				
Funnels, bowls, buckets, cups, and scoops				X	X		X		X
Shovels, rakes, sieves, sifters, and molds					X				X
Sponges, squirt bottles, and basters					X	X			X
Big Books						X			
Author/Illustrator/Artist Displays	X		X			X			
Reference Materials	X		X			X	X	X	X
Literature props (i.e., puppets, flannel board, flip charts)						X			
Story response sheets/charts						X		X	

Appendices

Print-related materials appear in italics. **Publishing/bookmaking materials appear in bold.**	Art	Blocks	Computer	Fine Motor	Housekeeping	Libarary/Listening	Math	Publishing	Science
Tape/CD player					X	X			
Story tapes/CDs and book(s)						X			
Song tapes/CDs (i.e., alphabet, number, concepts)						X			
Greeting cards, junk mail, and stationary					X			X	
Message board or class mailbox system								X	
Bingo/roll-on markers or sponge-top shoe polish								X	
Children's journals								X	
Pens, pencils/erasers, crayons, and markers	X	X	X	X	X	X	X	X	X
Notepads and paper of various sizes/colors	X	X	X	X	X	X	X	X	X
Story starters and motivational pictures								X	
Picture dictionary and children's thesaurus							X	X	X
Word bank, class list, and synonym/antonym charts								X	
Binding machine and plastic covers								X	
Plastic coins, paper money, and cash register					X		X		
Coin stamps and ink pad					X		X		
Analog/digital clock, sand/egg timers, and stop watch					X		X		X
Clock stamp and ink pad							X		X
Geometric plastic forms							X		
Fraction/tiles/circles							X		
Color tiles/wheel	X						X		X

145

A Young Writer's World

APPENDIX 3
The Writing Environment Checklist

1. **Books and Other Reading Materials**   YES   NO
   Do books reflect many interests? ____ ____
   Do books reflect different developmental levels? ____ ____
   Are books illustrated in a variety of ways? ____ ____
   Are there:
   > wordless picture books? ____ ____
   > information and content area books? ____ ____
   > biographies? ____ ____
   > plays or poetry selections? ____ ____
   > student-written books? ____ ____
   > magazines and newspapers appropriate for children? ____ ____
   > picture/story books? ____ ____
   > award winners (Caldecott, Children's Choice, ALA)? ____ ____
   > dictionaries or other reference books? ____ ____

2. **Supplies and Equipment for Recording Language**   YES   NO
   Are there pencils and paper for recording children's language? ____ ____
   Are tape recorders and/or computers used for recording language? ____ ____
   Are student journals used? ____ ____
   Is there a message center or mailbox system for communication? ____ ____

3. **Children's Work Displays**   YES   NO
   Are there various places that display children's work? ____ ____
   Do displays include children's writing? ____ ____
   Are children's projects with written explanations exhibited? ____ ____
   Is work from different children displayed? ____ ____
   Is current (less than two weeks old) work displayed? ____ ____

4. **Written Information**   YES   NO
   Are there notices, announcements, or a menu posted? ____ ____
   Is a daily schedule present? ____ ____
   Are calendar activities or weather charts used daily? ____ ____
   Are there sign-up sheets or daily attendance charts? ____ ____

5. **Signs, Labels, and Directions**   YES   NO
   Are key objects labeled? ____ ____
   Is there written language or pictures that provide instructions? ____ ____
   Is there written language or pictures that locate materials? ____ ____

Appendices

6. **Art Center**　　　　　　　　　　　　　　　　　　　　　　YES　NO
    - Do the materials foster hands-on exploration?　　　____　____
    - Is collaboration fostered?　　　____　____
    - Is oral language fostered?　　　____　____
    - Does the center contain writing materials?　　　____　____
    - Are books present?　　　____　____
    - Is environmental print included?　　　____　____
    - Are center-specific print-related materials present?　　　____　____
    - Is there at least one opportunity to write?　　　____　____

7. **Block Center**　　　　　　　　　　　　　　　　　　　　　YES　NO
    - Do the materials foster hands-on exploration?　　　____　____
    - Is collaboration fostered?　　　____　____
    - Is oral language fostered?　　　____　____
    - Does the center contain writing materials?　　　____　____
    - Are books present?　　　____　____
    - Is environmental print included?　　　____　____
    - Are center-specific print-related materials present?　　　____　____
    - Is there at least one opportunity to write?　　　____　____

8. **Computer Center**　　　　　　　　　　　　　　　　　　　YES　NO
    - Do the materials foster hands-on exploration?　　　____　____
    - Is collaboration fostered?　　　____　____
    - Is oral language fostered?　　　____　____
    - Does the center contain writing materials?　　　____　____
    - Are books present?　　　____　____
    - Is environmental print included?　　　____　____
    - Are center-specific print-related materials present?　　　____　____
    - Is there at least one opportunity to write?　　　____　____

9. **Fine Motor Center**　　　　　　　　　　　　　　　　　　YES　NO
    - Do the materials foster hands-on exploration?　　　____　____
    - Is collaboration fostered?　　　____　____
    - Is oral language fostered?　　　____　____
    - Does the center contain writing materials?　　　____　____
    - Are books present?　　　____　____
    - Is environmental print included?　　　____　____
    - Are center-specific print-related materials present?　　　____　____
    - Is there at least one opportunity to write?　　　____　____

APPENDIX 3
The Writing Environment Checklist (continued)

10. **Housekeeping Center**   YES   NO
    - Do the materials foster hands-on exploration?
    - Is collaboration and oral language fostered?
    - Does the center contain writing materials?
    - Are books present?
    - Is environmental print included?
    - Are center-specific print-related materials present?
    - Is there at least one opportunity to write?

11. **Library/Listening Center**   YES   NO
    - Do the materials foster hands-on exploration?
    - Is collaboration and oral language fostered?
    - Does the center contain writing materials?
    - Are books present?
    - Is environmental print included?
    - Are center-specific print-related materials present?
    - Is there at least one opportunity to write?

12. **Math Center**   YES   NO
    - Is it partitioned off from other areas in a quiet section the room?
    - Is it large enough to accommodate at least four children?
    - Is it attractive and inviting?
    - Is their an organizational system for locating books?
    - Are books displayed in a variety of ways, theme books grouped together?
    - Is there an element of softness (e. g., cushions, throw rugs, or pillows)?
    - Are posters or bulletin boards used to encourage and/or inform?
    - Are there any "literature props"?
    - Are there recordings of stories with accompanying book?
    - Do the story cassettes/CDs represent a variety of literature?

13. **Publishing Center**   YES   NO
    - Is there a space with tables or desks for writing?   ___   ___
    - Is there paper of various colors, shapes, and sizes?   ___   ___
    - Are there pre-made books of various shapes and sizes?   ___   ___
    - Are there book-making materials?   ___   ___
    - Is there a variety of writing instruments?   ___   ___
    - Is there chalk and chalkboard(s) or dry erase board(s) and markers?   ___   ___
    - Are there pictures and/or prompts to motivate writing?   ___   ___
    - Are there books, newspapers, or magazines to serve as writing models?   ___   ___
    - Are there stencils, stickers, rubber stamps, or letters to form words?   ___   ___
    - Are there dictionaries, word lists or word banks?   ___   ___
    - Is there a computer or typewriter?   ___   ___

14. **Science Center**   YES   NO
    - Do the materials foster hands-on exploration?   ___   ___
    - Are collaboration and oral language fostered?   ___   ___
    - Does the center contain writing materials?   ___   ___
    - Are books present?   ___   ___
    - Is environmental print included?   ___   ___
    - Are center-specific print-related materials present?   ___   ___
    - Is there at least one opportunity to write?   ___   ___

Appendix 3 is available in a digital format for easy printing at: ExchangePress.com/writer

APPENDIX 4
Scenarios and Props

Airline Ticket Counter
Cash register and receipts
Telephone, phone list, and message pad
Typewriter or computer
Credit cards, play money, and checks
Flight schedules and signs
Luggage tags and stickers
Maps and globes
Signs
Tickets and itineraries

Automobile Repair Shop
Car repair tools
Cash register and receipts
Coveralls or jump suits
Credit cards, play money, and checks
Magazines and newspapers (for waiting area)
Old car parts
Pens/pencils and message pads
Order forms, bills, and envelopes
Signs (shop name, hours, exit, safety posters)
Telephone, telephone book, and message pad
Wheeled scooter or underbody board

Car Dealership
Business cards for sales representatives
Cars made from large cardboard boxes
Dealership ads from newspaper
Magazines, brochures, and posters
Mirror with wax pencil (for writing
       and changing prices)
Pens, pencils, and paper
Receipt pads and special-order forms
Signs and posters
Telephone, telephone book, and message pad
Typewriter or computer
Calculator or adding machine
Window stickers

Fine Dining
Apron, pen, and order pad for waitstaff
Easel or chalkboard listing the daily specials
Gourmet magazines
Cash register and receipts
Credit cards, play money, and checks
Menus
Paper and pens for writing food reviews
Sign displaying name and hours

Tablecloth, napkins, dishes, and silverware
Tables and chairs

Grocery Store
Cash register
Employee vests and nametags
Clean, empty food boxes and containers
Coupons
Newspaper grocery ads
Paper and plastic bags
Plastic foods
Play money, credit cards, and checks
Price signs and daily specials
Receipts
Recipe cards
Scale for weighing produce
Shopper's club cards and applications
Shopping carts and baskets
Sign displaying store name and hours

Hairdresser Center
Brush and comb
Hair dryer (cordless)
Empty shampoo bottle
Ribbons, barrettes, clips, and hair rollers
Wig and wig stand
Mirror
Curling iron (cordless)
Posters and magazines of hairstyles
Open/closed sign
Towel
Appointment book, calendar, and pens
Telephone, telephone book, and message pad

Library
A sign-in/sign-out sheet file folder
A wide variety of children's books
Telephone, telephone book, and message pad
Bookmarks
Signs
Self-adhesive note pads and stickers
Paper of assorted sizes
Posters of children's books
Flyers for upcoming events
Date stamp and inkpad for
       checking out books
ABC index cards
Typewriter or computer

Medical Center
Calendar, appointment books, and pens
Dolls (for patients)
Folders (for patient records)
Medical bag
Prescription pad and pens
Stethoscope, thermometer,
 and child-safe tweezers
White shirt/jacket and nametags
Assorted bandages (adhesive and cloth)
Tongue depressors, cotton swabs,
 and cotton balls
Eye chart and posters
Magazines and newspapers (for waiting area)

Office
Appointment book and calendar
Books, pamphlets, magazines
Clipboards
Business cards
File cabinet
In/out trays and trays for holding small items
Assorted forms, ledgers, and folders
Post-its/address labels and envelopes
Pens, pencils, markers, paper, and cards
Telephone, telephone book,
 and message pad
Office supplies
Signs (e.g., open, closed, exit)
Typewriter or computer keyboard

Pizzeria
Aprons and chef's hat
Cash register and receipts
Chart displaying pizza sizes
Cups, plates, plastic silverware, and napkins
Coupons and ad flyers
Menus and daily specials
Pens/pencils and order pads
Pizza boxes
Play money, credit cards, and checks
Rebus recipes for various types of pizzas
Rolling pins, pans, and pie cutters
Shakers for peppers and cheese
Signs
Telephone, telephone book, and message pad
Toppings (cut from solid, vinyl place mats)

Post Office
A tote bag for mail
Assorted forms
Calendars of various sizes
Cash register and receipts
Credit cards, play money, and checks
Envelopes, small boxes, and labels
 of various sizes
Pens, pencils, markers
Mailbox (made from a cardboard box)
Posters/signs about mailing
Stationery, stickers, stamps, stamp pads

Theater
Cash register
Concession stand props
Flashlight for ushers
Marquis outside theater
Menu and price lists for concessions
Name tags for workers
Numbered pillows arranged for seating
Play money, credit cards, and checks
Playbill and/or programs
Posters advertising the current show
Price lists for tickets
Prop/costumes
Receipts
Scripts for short stories
 (including pictures and words)
Small stage or puppet theater
Theater signs (Exit, No Smoking,
 or Quiet Please)
Ticket window and tickets with numbers

Travel Agency
Business cards for agents
Calendar
Computer or typewriter
Magazines, brochures, and travel posters
Maps and/or globe
Tickets and itineraries
Signs
Tables and chairs
Telephone, telephone book, and message pad

TV Weather Studio
"On Air" sign
Cardboard box cameras
Cue cards, blank cards, and markers
Desk and chairs
Microphone
Pointers
Tape recorder
Typewriter, pens/pencils, and paper
 (for writing scripts)
Various maps

APPENDIX 5
Discovery Boxes by Theme

Apples
Books: Apples by Gail Gibbons; How Do Apples Grow? by Betsy and Giulio Maestro; Apples for Everyone by Jill Esbaum; Apples, Apples, Apples by Nancy Elizabeth Wallace; and Ten Red Apples by Pat Hutchins.

Materials: several apples of different varieties, apple seeds, pieces of dried apple, and a magnifying glass.

Bones
Books: Bone by Bone: Comparing Animal Skeletons by Sara Levine and T. S. Spookytooth; The Skeleton Inside You by Philip Balestrino and True Kelley; Bend and Stretch: Learning About Your Bones and Muscles by Pamela Hill Nettleton and Becky Shipe; and Dem Bones by Bob Barner.

Materials: cleaned bones*, x-rays, pictures of small skeletons from different animals, black paper, chalk, styrofoam peanuts, and toothpicks. (*Save chicken bones or ask your local zoo or veterinarian to donate bones. Then, boil them or place them in a bleach solution to kill germs.)

Buttons
Books: The Button Box by Margarette S. Reid and Sarah Chamberlin; The Button Box by Janet Sever Hull and Vicki Kiljon Guess; Grandma's Button Box by Linda William Aber; and A Button Story by Emil Sher and Cindy Revell.

Materials: assorted buttons, sorting tray, magnifying glass, balance scale, and twine or thin cord (for stringing).

Coins
Books: Lots and Lots of Coins by Margarette S. Reid and True Kelley; The Penny Pot by Stuart Murphy; The Coin Counting Book by Rozanne Lanczak Williams; and Once Upon a Dime: A Math Adventure by Nancy Kelly Allen and Adam Doyle.

Materials: assorted coins from different countries, sorting trays, magnifying glass, newsprint and unwrapped crayons (to make rubbings), and a balance scale.

Color
Books: Around the Color Wheel by Debbie Barry; Pantone: Colors by Pantone; Color Zoo by Lois Ehlert; Mouse Paint by Ellen Stoll Walsh; A Color of His Own by Leo Lionni; and Little Blue and Little Yellow by Leo Lionni.

Materials: color wheel; translucent plastic color paddles; paint color samples; and red, yellow, and blue modeling dough (for mixing).

Gadgets
Books: Mad Gadget by Chris Winn; The Everything Machine by Matt Novak; and Rosie Revere, Engineer by Andrea Beaty and David Roberts.

Materials: assorted screw drivers, nonworking small appliances (such as a clock, radio, tape recorder, mixer, or rotary telephone—avoid TVs or computer monitors).

Insects
Books: The Bug Book by Sue Fliess; Bugs A to Z by Caroline Lawton; and What is an Insect?, What Do Insects Do?, and Where Do Insects Live? all by Susan Canizares.

Materials: a variety of real and plastic insects, a view sphere and/or hand lens, and child-safe tweezers.

Leaves
Books: Fall is Not Easy by Marty Kelley; Tops and Bottoms by Janet Stevens; Autumn Leaves by Ken Robbins; Red Leaf, Yellow Leaf by Lois Ehlert; Look What I Did With a Leaf! by Morteza E. Sohi; Leaf by Leaf: Autumn Poems selected by Barbara Rogasky; and Fall Leaves Fall! by Zoe Hall.

Materials: real and artificial leaves of various shapes, sizes, and colors; a magnifying glass; and newsprint and unwrapped crayons (to make rubbings).

Appendices

Marbles
Books: Marbles: A Player's Guide by Shar Levine and Vicki Scudamore; *Penny and her Marble* by Kevin Henkes; and *Playing Marbles: Story and Pictures* by Julie Brinckloe.

Materials: assorted marbles, several small plastic containers, loops made from yarn or string, and foam pipe insulation (available at a home improvement store) cut into varying lengths and halved to produce chutes.

Measuring
Books: Inchworm and a Half by Elinor J. Pinczes and Randall Enos; *How Big is a Foot?* by Rolf Myle; *How Tall? Wacky Ways to Compare Height* by Mark Weakland and Igor Sinkovec; and *How Long? Wacky Ways to Compare Length* by Jessica Gunderson.

Materials: a set of measuring feet (cut from vinyl placements numbered 1-10); flexible, vinyl tape measure; rulers; and self-retracting tape measures.

Pumpkins
Books: The Pumpkin Book by Gail Gibbons; *From Seed to Pumpkin* by Wendy Pfeffer and James Graham Hale; *Seed, Sprout, Pumpkin, Pie* by Jill Esbaum; *Pumpkin Light* by David Ray; *Plumply, Dumply Pumpkin* by Mary Serfozo and Valeria Petrone; and *Pumpkin Soup* by Helen Cooper.

Materials: small pumpkins of various colors, shapes, and sizes; flexible, vinyl tape measure; small, kitchen; and pumpkin seeds.

Ramps
Books: Roll, Slope, and Slide: A Book about Ramps by Michael Dahl and Denise Shea; and *Simple Machines: Wheels, Levers and Pulleys* by David A. Adler and Anna Raff.

Materials: thin strips of wooden board (for ramps), small wooden blocks (for elevating boards), toy cars, and a stop watch.

Reflection
Books: The Magic Mirror Book by Marion Walter; *Light: Shadows, Mirrors, and Rainbows*; and *Mirror* by Sandhya Rao and Ashok Rajag.

Materials: a variety of mirrors (flat, flexible, hinged), metal spoons, foil, and shiny ornamental Christmas balls and other non-breakable items with a reflective surface.

Rocks
Books: Remarkable Rocks by Ron Cole; *A Rock is Lively* by Dianna Aston and Sylvia Long; *What Happens to Rock?* by Fred Biddulph; *Investigating Rocks* by Natalie Lunis and Nancy White; *National Geographic Readers: Rocks and Minerals* by Kathleen Weidner Zoehfeld; *Using Rocks* by Alfredo Schifini; and *Rocks: Hard, Soft, Smooth, and Rough* by Natalie M. Rosinsky and Matthew John.

Materials: a collection of rocks with a variety of sizes, colors, and textures, including fossils, fool's gold, polished rocks, and geodes; sorting trays; a magnifying glass; and a balance scale.

Seashells
Books: Shells: The Photographic Recognition Guide to Seashells of the World by S. Peter Dance; *Seashells* by Josie Iselin and Sandy Carlson; *Seashells by the Seashore* by Marianne Berkes and Robert Noreika; *It's a Seashell Day* by Dianne Ochiltree and Elliot Kreloff; and *What Lives in a Shell?* by Kathleen Zoehfeld and Helen Davie.

Materials: a collection of seashells with a variety of sizes, shapes, color, and texture; sorting trays; magnifying glass; and a balance scale.

Seeds
Books: A Seed is Sleepy by Dianna Aston and Sylvia Long; *National Geographic Readers: Seed to Plant* by Kristin Baird Rattini; *Ten Seeds* by Ruth Brown; *From Seed to Plant* by Gail Gibbons; and *Seeds* by Ken Robbins.

Materials: seeds from plants and trees (i.e., oranges seeds, apple seeds, acorns, burrs, umbrella seeds, pods, beans, peas, dried corn, milkweed, chestnuts, poppy seeds, apricot pits, peach pits), sorting trays, and hand lenses or a jeweler's loop.

APPENDIX 6
Learning Center Book Lists

Art Center

Anholt, Laurence. *Camille and the Sunflowers: A Story About Vincent van Gogh*. London: Frances Lincoln Limited, 1994.

Björk, Christina. *Linnea in Monet's Garden*. Stockholm, R & S Books, 1987.

Carle, Eric. *The Artists Who Painted a Blue Horse*. New York, NY: Philomel Books, 2011.

Chicago Historical Society. *ABC History Mystery*. Chicago, IL: Chicago Historical Society, 2000.

dePaola, Tomie. *The Art Lesson*. New York, NY: Scholastic, 1989.

Greenberg, Jan and Sandra Jordan. *Action Jackson*. New York, NY: Square Fish, 2002.

Laden, Nina. *When Piagasso Met Mootisse*. San Francisco, CA: Chronicle Books, 1998.

Lithgow, John. *Micawber*. New York, NY: Simon and Schuster Children's Publishing, 2002.

Metropolitan Museum of Art. *Museum ABC*. New York, NY: Little, Brown and Company, 2002.

Micklethwait, Lucy. *I Spy: An Alphabet in Art*. New York, NY: Greenwillow Books, 1992.

Micklethwait, Lucy. *I Spy Two Eyes: Numbers In Art*. New York: Greenwillow Books, 1993.

Weitzman, Jacqueline Preiss. *You Can't Take a Balloon into the Metropolitan Museum of Art. You Can't Take a Balloon into the National Gallery. You Can't Take a Balloon into the Museum of Fine Arts*. New York, NY: Puffin Books. 2000, 2001, 2002.

Block Center

Alling, Niki. *When I Build with Blocks*. Scotts Valley, CA: CreateSpace Independent Publishing Platform, 2012.

Barton, Byron. *Building a House*. New York, NY: William Morrow and Company, 1981.

Beaty, Andrea. *Iggy Peck, Architect*. New York, NY: Harry N. Abrams, 2007.

Buchanan, Ken. *This House is Made of Mud*. Cleveland, OH: Northland Publishing, 1994.

Carle, Eric. *A House for Hermit Crab*. New York, NY: Simon & Schuster, 2002.

Fleming, Denise. *Alphabet Under Construction*. New York, NY: Henry Holt and Company, 2002.

Gibbons, Gail. *How a House Is Built*. New York, NY: Holiday House, 1996.

Gibbons, Gail. *Up Goes the Skyscraper!* New York, NY: Simon and Schuster, 1990.

Hoberman, Mary Ann. *A House Is a House for Me*. New York, NY: Penguin, 1982.

Hutchins, Pat. *Changes, Changes*. New York, NY: Simon and Schuster, 1987.

Jackson, Thomas Campbell. *Hammers, Nails, Planks, and Paint: How a House Is Built*. New York, NY: Scholastic, 1994.

Johnson, Stephen T. *Alphabet City*. And *City by Numbers*. New York, NY: Penguin, 2003.

Klove, Lars. *Trucks that Build*. New York, NY: Simon and Schuster, 2000.

Lewis, Kevin. *The Lot at the End of My Block*. New York, NY: Hyperion Books for Children, 2001.

Macaulay, David. Cathedral: *The Story of Its Construction*. And *Pyramid* and *Castle*. Boston, MA: Houghton Mifflin, 1973 and 1975.

Merriam, Eve. *Bam Bam Bam*. New York, NY: Henry Holt, 1998.

Sobel, June. *B Is for Bulldozer: A Construction ABC*. Boston, MA: Houghton Mifflin, 2003.

Steele, Philip. *House: Through the Ages*. Mahwah, NJ: Troll Associates, 1994.

Stevenson, Robert Louis. *Block City*. New York, NY: Penguin, 1988

Suen, Anastasia. *Raise the Roof*. New York, NY: Penguin, 2003.

Tarsky, Sue. *The Busy Building Book*. New York, NY: Penguin, 1997.

Van Dusen, Chris. *If I Built a House*. New York, NY: Penguin, 2012.

Whitehouse, Patricia. *What Can Build?* Portsmouth, NH: Heinemann, 2004.

Computer Center
Anders, "Dr. Hope" Tim. *Chip, The Little Computer*. Fallbrook, CA: Alpine Publishing, 1999.

Bedford, David. *Once Upon a Time...Online: Happily Ever After Is Only a Click Away!* Barrington, IL: Parragon, 2016.

Bueno, Carlos. *Lauren Ipsum: A Story About Computer Science and Other Improbable Things*. San Francisco, CA: No Starch Press, 2014.

Buzzeo, Toni. *But I Read It on the Internet! (Mrs. Skorupski Story)*. Madison, WI: Upstart Books, 2013.

Collins, Suzanne. *When Charlie McButton Lost Power*. New York, NY: Penguin, 2007.

Cook, Julia. *The Technology Tail: A Digital Footprint Story (Communicate with Confidence)*. Boys Town, NE: Boys Town Press, 2017.

Droyd, Ann. *If You Give a Mouse an iPhone: A Cautionary Tale*. New York, NY: Penguin, 2014.

Liukas, Linda. *Hello Ruby: Adventures in Coding*. New York, NY: Feiwel & Friends, 2015.

Liukas, Linda. *Hello Ruby: Journey Inside the Computer*. New York, NY: Feiwel & Friends, 2017.

Willis, Jeanne. *Chicken Clicking*. London, England: Andersen Press, 2014.

Math Center
Counting Books
Archambault, John. *Counting Sheep*. Illustrated by John Rombola. New York, NY: Henry Holt & Co., 1989.

Archambault, John. *Baby's First Counting Book*. New York, NY: Platt & Munk, 1988.

Aylesworth, Jim. *One Crow*. Philadelphia, PA: Lippincott Williams & Wilkins, 1988.

Bang, Molly. *Ten, Nine, Eight*. New York, NY: Greenwillow Books, 1983.

Blumenthal, Nancy. *Count-a-saurus*. New York, NY: Macmillian Publishing, 1989.

Bright, Robert. *My Red Umbrella*. New York, NY: William Morrow, 1985.

Bucknall, Caroline, *One Bear All Alone*. New York, NY: Penguin, 1985.

Calmenson, Stephanie. *One Little Monkey*. New York, NY: Parents Magazine Press, 1982.

Carle, Eric. *1, 2, 3 to the Zoo*. New York, NY: Philomel Books, 1990.

Carter, David A. *How Many Bugs in a Box?* New York, NY: Simon & Schuster, 1988.

Chandler, Jean. *The Poky Little Puppy's Counting Book*. Racine, WI: Western Publishing Co., 1980.

Corbett, Grahame. *What Number Now?* New York, NY: Dial Books for Young Readers, 1982.

APPENDIX 6
Learning Center Book Lists (continued)

Math Center (continued)
Counting Books

Davis, Jim. *Garfield Counts to Ten.* New York, NY: Random House, 1983.

Day, Nancy Raines and Kurt Cyrus. *What in the World? Numbers in Nature.* San Diego, CA: Beach Lane Books, 2015.

Ernst, Lisa Campbell. *Up to Ten and Down Again.* New York, NY: Lothrop, Lee & Shepard Books, 1986.

Feelings, Muriel. *Moja Means One (Swahili Counting Book).* New York, NY: Dial Books for Young Readers. 1985.

Friskey, Margaret. *Chicken Little, Count-to-Ten.* Chicago, IL: Children's Press, 1946.

Gerstein, Mordicai. *Roll Over.* New York, NY: Dial Books for Young Readers, 1985.

Gillham, Bill, and Susan Hulme. *Let's Look for Numbers.* New York, NY: Corward-McCann, 1984.

Goldborough, June. *Numbers.* Teaneck, N.J.: Sharon Publications, 1983.

Gretz, Susanna. *Ten Green Bottles.* New York, NY: Puffin Books, 1976.

Gundersheimer, Karen. *1 2 3 Play with Me.* New York, NY: Harper & Row Publishers, 1984.

Haas, Dorothy. *The Hugs and Tugs Counting Book.* Beverly, MA: Parker Brothers Publishing, 1984.

Haskins, Jim. *Count Your Way Through China.* Minneapolis, MN: Carolrhoda Books, 1988.

Hoban, Tana. *1,2,3.* New York, NY: Greenwillow Books, 1985.

Hoban, Tana. *Count and See.* New York, NY: Simon & Schuster Children's Publishing, 1972.

Hoban, Tana. *More Than One.* New York, NY: William Morrow & Co., 1981.

Hooper, Meridith. *Seven Eggs.* New York, NY: Harperfestival, 1992.

Hughes, Shirley. *When We Went to the Park.* New York, NY: Lothrop, Lee & Shepard Book, 1985.

Hutchins, Pat. *One Hunter.* New York, NY: Greenwillow Books, 1982.

Ilse-Margret Vogel. *1 is No Fun But 20 is Plenty.* Eau Claire, WI: E.M. Hale, 1969.

Inkpen, Mike. *One Bear at Bedtime.* Boston, MA: Little, Brown & Co., 1987.

Johnston, Tony. *Whale Song.* New York, NY: G.P. Putnam's Sons, 1987.

Katz, Bobbi. *Ten Little Care Bears Counting Book.* New York, NY: Random House, 1983.

Kessler, Ethel and Leonard. *Two, Four, Six, Eight (A Book About Legs).* New York, NY: Dodd Mead, 1980.

Killingback, Julia. *One, Two, Three, Go!* New York, NY: William Morrow, 1985.

Kitamura, Satashi. *When Sheep Cannot Sleep.* New York, NY: Farrar, Straus and Giroux, 1988.

Knight, Hilary. *The Twelve Days of Christmas.* New York, NY: Simon & Schuster Children's Publishing, 2001.

Le Sieg, Theo. *Ten Apples Up on Top.* New York, NY: Beginner Books, 1961.

Lynn, Sara, and Rosalinda Kightley. *1 2 3.* Boston, MA: Little, Brown & Co., 1986.

MacDonald, Elizabeth. *Mike's Kite*. New York, NY: Orchard Books, 1990.

MacDonald, Suse, and Bill Oakes. *Numbers*. New York, NY: Dial Books for Young Readers, 1988.

McMillan, Bruce. *Counting Wildflowers*. New York, NY: William Morrow, 1995.

Matthias, Catherine. *Too Many Balloons*. Chicago, IL: Children's Press, 1982.

Micklethwait, L. *I Spy Two Eyes: Numbers in Art*. New York: Greenwillow Books, 1993.

Miller, Jane. *Farm Counting Book*. New York, NY: William Morrow, 1995.

Miller, J.P. *Learn to Count with Little Rabbit*. New York, NY: Random House, 1984.

Moncure, Jane Belk. *Magic Monsters Count to Ten*. Elgin, IL: Child's World, 1979.

Morozumi, Atsuko. *One Gorilla*. New York, NY: Farrar, Straus & Giroux, 1990.

Morris, Ann. *Night Counting*. New York, NY: Harper & Row Publishers, 1986.

Noll, Sally. *Off and Counting*. New York, NY: Greenwillow Books, 1984.

Oxenbury, Helen. *Numbers of Things*. New York, NY: William Morrow, 1995.

Petty, Kate and Lisa Kopper. *What's That Number?* New York, NY: Franklin Watts, 1986.

Pye, Sylvia E. Luckas. *Counting Animals with Jack: A 1-10 Number Picture Book*. New York, NY: Vantage Press, 1987.

Russell, Sandra. *A Farmer's Dozen*. New York, NY: HarperCollins Publishers. 1982.

Schade, Susan. *The Noisy Counting Book*. New York, NY: Random House, 1987.

Sendak, Maurice. *One Was Johnny*. New York, NY: HarperTrophy, 1991.

Serfozo, Mary. *Who Wants One?* New York, NY: Margaret K. McElderry, 1989.

Stobbs, Joanna and William. *One Sun, Two Eyes, and a Million Stars*. Oxford, England: Oxford University Press Children's Books, 1983.

Sullivan, C. *Numbers at Play: A Counting Book*. New York, NY: Rizzoli International Publications, 1992.

Tafuri, Nancy. *Who's Counting?* New York, NY: Greenwillow Books, 1986.

Tester, Sylvia R. *One Unicorn: A Counting Book*. Elgin, IL: Child's World, 1977.

Thompson, Susan L. *One More Thing, Dad*. Morton Grove, Ill.: Albert Whitman, 1980.

Trinca, Rod. *One Wooly Wornbat*. La Jolla, CA: Kane/Miller Book Publishers, 1987.

Tudor, Tasha. *1 is One*. New York, NY: Simon & Schuster Children's Publishing, 2000.

Wadsworth, Olive. *Over in the Meadow*. New York, NY: North-South Books, 2002.

Wells, Rosemary. *Max's Toys: A Counting Book*. New York, NY: Dial Books for Young Readers, 1979.

Wildsmith, Brian. *Brian Wildsmith's 1, 2, 3's*. New York, NY: Franklin Watts, 1973.

Wood, A.J. *Animal Counting*. Los Angeles, CA: Price/Stern/Sloan Publishers, 1987.

Woodard, James and Linda Purdy. *One to Ten and Count Again*. La Puente, CA: Jay Alden Publishers, 1972.

Yoeman, John. *Sixes and Sevens*. New York, NY: Macmillan Publishing Co., 1974.

Yolen, Jane. *An Invitation to the Butterfly Ball*. New York, NY: Boyds Mills Press, 1997.

APPENDIX 6
Learning Center Book Lists *(continued)*

Math Center (continued)

Adler, David. *Place Value.* New York, NY: Holiday House, 2017.

Burns, Marilyn. *Spaghetti and Meatballs for All! A Mathematical Story.* New York, NY: Scholastic, 2008.

Christelow, Eileen. *Five Little Monkeys Jumping on the Bed.* New York, NY: Scholastic, 1989.

Cleary, Brian. *The Action of Subrtraction.* Minneapolis, MN: Millbrook Press, 2008.

Cristaldi, Kathryn. *Even Steven and Odd Todd.* New York, NY: Cartwheel, 1996.

Dodds, Dayle Ann. *Full House: An Invitation to Fractions.* Somerville, MA: Candlewick Press, 2009.

Grossman, Virginia. *Ten Little Rabbits.* San Francisco, CA: Chronicle Books, 1991.

Hutchins, Pat. *The Doorbell Rang.* New York, NY: Scholastic, 1987.

Long, Lynette. *Domino Addition.* Watertown, MA: Charlesbridge Publishing, 1996.

LoPresti, Angeline Sparagna. *A Place For Zero.* Watertown, MA: Charlesbridge, 2003.

McGrath, Barbara Barbieri. *The M&M's Brand Chocolate Candies Counting Book.* Watertown, MA: Charlesbridge, 1994.

McMillian, Bruce. *Jelly Beans for Sale.* New York, NY: Scholastic, 1998.

McMillan, Bruce. *One, Two, One Pair!* New York, NY: Scholastic, 1991.

Miranda, Anne. *Monster Math.* Boston, MA: HMH Books for Young Readers, 2002.

Murphy, Stuart. *Animals on Board (MathStart 2).* New York, NY: HarperCollins, 1998.

Murphy, Stuart. *Double the Ducks (MathStart 1).* New York, NY: HarperCollins, 2002.

Pallotta, Jerry. *The Hershey's Milk Chocolate Bar Fractions Book.* New York, NY: Scholastic, 1999.

Pallotta, Jerry. *Reese's Pieces Count by Fives.* New York, NY: Scholastic, 2000.

Pallotta, Jerry. *Twizzlers Percentages Book.* New York, NY: Scholastic, 2001.

Pinczes, Elinor J. *One Hundred Hungry Ants.* New York, NY: Scholastic, 1997.

Ryan, Pam Munoz and Jerry Pallotta. *The Crayon Counting Book.* Watertown, MA: Charlesbridge, 1996.

Schlein, Miriam. *More Than One.* New York, NY: Scholastic, 1997.

Shaskan, Trisha Speed. *If You Were a Minus Sign (Math Fun).* Mankato, MN: Picture Window Books, 2008.

Walton, Rick. *How Many How Many How Many.* Cambridge, MA: Candlewick Press, 1993.

Williams, Rozanne Lanczak. *The Coin Counting Book.* New York, NY: Scholastic, 2002.

Ziefert, Harriet. *A Dozen Dozen Eggs.* New York, NY: Viking, 1998.

Science Center
See Appendix 5 Discovery Boxes by Theme for additional titles.

Appendices

NOTES

Introduction
1. Brian Cambourne, *The Whole Story: Natural Learning and the Acquisition of Literacy in the Classroom* (Auckland, New Zealand: Ashton Scholastic, 1988).

2. Karen W. Tunks and Rebecca M. Giles, *Write Now! Publishing with Young Authors, Prekindergarten through Second Grade* (Portsmouth, NH: Heinemann, 2007).

Chapter 1: Setting the Stage
1. Judith E. Kieff and Renee M. Casbergue, *Playful Learning and Teaching: Integrating Play into Preschool and Primary Programs* (Boston, MA: Allyn and Bacon, 2000).

2. National Association for the Education of Young Children & National Council of Teachers of Mathematics. *Early Childhood Mathematics: Promoting Good Beginnings* (Washington, D.C.: NAEYC, 2010).

Chapter 2: Playing with Print
1. S. J. Britsch and D. R. Meier, "Building a Literacy Community: The Role of Literacy and Social Practice in Early Childhood Programs," *Early Childhood Education Journal*, 26(4), 1999, 209-215.

2. D.S. Strickland and L.M. Morrow, "Environments Rich in Print Promote Literacy Behavior During Play," *Reading Teacher*, 43(4), 1988, 330-331.

3. C. Vukelich and C. Valentine, "A Child Plays: Two Teachers Learn," *Reading Teacher*, 44(4), 1990, 342-344.

4. C. Vukelich, "Where's the Paper? Literacy During Dramatic Play," *Childhood Education*, 67, 1990, 205-209.

5. S. B. Neuman and K. Roskos, "Play, Print and Purpose: Enriching Play Environments for Literacy Development," *Reading Teacher*, 44(3), 1990, 214-221.

6. S. B. Neuman and K. Roskos, "Whatever Happened to Developmentally Appropriate Practices in Literacy?" *Young Children*, 60, 2005, 1–6.

7. J. E. Stroud, J.E. "Block Play: Building a Foundation for Literacy," *Early Childhood Education Journal*, 23(1), 1995, 9-13.

8. M. C. Fadool, "'We Don't Serve No Ice Cream!': Enhancing Children's Understanding and Use of Literacy Through Play Events," *Journal of Reading Education*, 34(3), 2009, 23–29.

9. A. D. Pellegrini, "Relations Between Preschool Children's Symbolic Play and Literate Behavior" (pp. 79-97) In L. Galda & A. D. Pellegrini (Eds.) *Play, Language, and Stories: The Development of Literate Behavior* (Norwood, NJ: Ablex, 1985).

10. S. Neuman and K. Roskos, "Peers as Literacy Informants: A Description of Young Children's Literacy Conversations in Play" *Early Childhood Research Quarterly*, 6(2), 1991, 233-248.

11. Y. Tsao, "Using Guided Play to Enhance Children's Conversation, Creativity and Competence in Literacy," *Education*, 128(3), 2008, 515–520.

12. Elinor Goldschmied, Ruth Forbes and Sonia Jackson, *People Under Three, Young Children in Day Care* (rev 3rd ed.) (London & New York: Routledge, 2004).

13. Brian Cambourne, *The Whole Story: Natural Learning and the Acquisition of Literacy in the Classroom* (Auckland, New Zealand: Ashton Scholastic, 1988).

14. L.S. Vygotsky, "Play and Its Role in the Mental Development of the Child," *Soviet Psychology*, 12, 1966, 67-76.

Chapter 3: Plenty of Print

1. Y. Goodman, "Children Coming to Know Literacy" in W.H. Teale & E. Sulzby (Eds.), *Emergent Literacy: Writing and Reading.* (Norwood, NJ: Ablex, 1986). L.M. McGee and D.J Richgels, *Literacy's Beginnings: Supporting Young Readers and Writers* (3rd ed.). (Boston, MA: Allyn & Bacon 2000). W.H. Teale, "Home Background and Young Children's Literacy Development" in W.H. Teale and E. Sulzby (Eds.), *Emergent Literacy: Writing and Reading.* (Norwood, NJ: Ablex, 1986).

2. M. Clay, *An Observation Survey of Early Literacy Achievement* (Portsmouth, NH: Heinemann, 1993).

Chapter 3: Plenty of Print *(continued)*

3. A.S. Epstein, "Helping Preschool Children Become Readers: Tips for Parents," *High/Scope ReSource*, Summer, 2002, 4–6.

4. D.Z. Kassow, "Environmental Print Awareness in Young Children," *Talaris*, 2006, 1(3).

5. J. Christie, B. Enz, M. Han, J. Prior and M. Gerard, "Effects of Environmental Print on Young Children's Print Recognition" In D. Sluss & O. Jarrett (Eds.), *Investigating Play in the 21st Century* (pp. 220-228). (Lanham, MD: University Press of America, 2007).

Chapter 4: Publishing Possibilities

1. Karen W. Tunks and Rebecca M. Giles, *Write Now! Publishing with Young Authors, Prekindergarten through Second Grade.* (Portsmouth, NH: Heinemann, 2007).

2. E. Sulzby, "Research Directions: Transitions from Emergent to Conventional Writing," *Language Arts*, 69(4), 1992, 290-97.

3. D.W. Rowe and C. Neitzel, "Interest and Agency in 2- and 3-Year-Olds' Participation in Emergent Writing," *Reading Research Quarterly* 45 (2), 2010, 169–95. L.R. Dennis and N.K. Votteler, "Preschool Teachers and Children's Emergent Writing: Supporting Diverse Learners," *Early Childhood Education Journal*, 41(6), 2013, 439–46.

4. A.H. Hall, A. Simpson, Y. Guo, and S. Wang, "Examining the Effects of Preschool Writing Instruction on Emergent Literacy Skills: A Systematic Review of the Literature," *Literacy Research and Instruction*, 52(2), 2015, 115-132.

5. G. Ouellette and M. Sénéchal, "Invented Spelling in Kindergarten as a Predictor of Reading and Spelling in Grade 1: A New Pathway to Literacy, or Just the Same Road, Less Known?" *Developmental Psychology*, 53(1), 2017, 77-88.

6. S. Graham, A. Gillespie and D. McKeown, D., "Writing: Importance, Development, and Instruction," *Reading & Writing*, 26(1), 2013, 1-15.

Chapter 5: Adult Writing Role Models

1. N.P. Gallavan, F.A. Bowles and C.T. Young, "Learning to Write and Writing to Learn: Insights from Teacher Candidates," *Action in Teacher Education*, 29(2), 2007, 61-69.

2. J. Bourne, "'Oh what will miss say!' Constructing Texts and Identities in the Discursive Processes of Classroom Writing," *Language and Education*, 16(4), 2002, 241-259. M. Ryan and G. Barton, "The Spatialized Practices of Teaching Writing in Elementary Schools: Diverse Students Shaping Discoursal Selves," *Research in the Teaching of English*, 48(3), 2014, 303-328.

3. R. Andrews, *The Case for a National Writing Project for Teachers* (Reading, England: CfBT Education Trust, 2008).

BIBLIOGRAPHY

Adams, M. J. *Beginning to Read: Thinking About Learning and Print.* Cambridge, MA: NUT Press, 1990.

Aldridge, J. T., & Rust, D. A beginning reading strategy. *Academic Therapy*, 22(3), 323-326, 1987.

Aliki. *How a Book Is Made.* New York, NY: Harper Collins, 1988.

Anderson, G. T., Spainhower, A. R., & Sharp, A. C. "Where do bears go?" The value of child-directed play. *Young Children*, 69(2), 8-14, 2014.

Banerjee, R., Alsalman, A. & Alqafari, S. Supporting sociodramatic play in preschools to promote language and literacy skills of English Language Learners. *Early Childhood Education Journal*, 44(4), 299-305, 2016.

Behymer, A. Kindergarten writing workshop. *The Reading Teacher*, 57(1), 85-88, 2003.

Bodrova, E. Make-believe play versus academic skills: A Vygotskian approach to today's dilemma of early childhood education. *European Early Childhood Education Research Journal*, 16(3), 357–369, 2008.

Bodrova, E., & Leong, D. J. Building language & literacy through PLAY. *Early Childhood Today*, 18(2), 34, 2003.

Bouley-Picard, T. M. Preservice teachers and preschoolers: The development of thematic literacy play centers. *Journal of Early Childhood Teacher Education*, 25(3), 211-222, 2005.

Britsch, S.J. & Meier, D.R. Building a literacy community: The role of literacy and social practice in early childhood programs. *Early Childhood Education Journal*, 26(4), 209-215, 1999.

Calkins, L. *The Art of Teaching Writing.* New ed. Portsmouth, NH: Heinemann, 1994.

Chall, J. *Stages of Reading Development* (2nd ed.). Fort Worth, TX: Harcourt Brace, 1996.

Bibliography

Clay, M. *An Observation Survey of Early Literacy Achievement*. Portsmouth, NH: Heinemann, 1993.

Clay, M. *Becoming Literate: The Construction of Inner Control*. Portsmouth, NH: Heinemann, 1991.

Cloer, T., Aldridge, J., & Dean, R. Examining different levels of print awareness. *Journal of Language Experience*, 4(1&2), 25-33, 1981/1982.

Crews, Donald. *School Bus*. New York, NY. Harper Collins, 1984.

Crosser, S. Making the most of sand play. *EarlyChildhoodNEWS*, 2008.

Cunningham, P. Want to teach basic skills? Try brand-name phonics! *Instructor*, 105 (5), 44-45, 1998.

Dunst, C. J., Simkus, A., & Hamby, D. W. Children's story retelling as a literacy and language enhancement strategy. *CELLreviews*, 5,(2). Asheville, NC: Orelena Hawks Puckett Institute, Center for Early Literacy Learning, 2012.

Durkin, D. *Children Who Read Early*. New York, NY: Teachers College Press, 1966.

Goodman, Y. Children coming to know literacy. In W.H. Teale & E. Sulzby (Eds.), *Emergent Literacy: Writing and Reading* (p. 1-14). Norwood, NJ: Ablex, 1986.

Gallavan, N. P., Bowles, F. A., & Young, C. T. Learning to write and writing to learn: Insights from teacher candidates. *Action in Teacher Education*, 29(2), 61-69, 2007.

Gibbons, Gail. *How a House Is Built*. New York, NY: Holiday House, 1990.

Giles, R. M., & Tunks, K. W. Putting power in action. *Texas Child Care Quarterly*, 33(1), 28-35, 2009.

Giles, R. M., & Tunks, K. W. Children write their world: Environmental print as a teaching tool. *Dimensions of Early Childhood*, 38(3), 23-29, 2010.

Giles, R. M., & Tunks, K. W. Outdoor authors: Publishing possibilities on the playground and beyond. *Exchange*, 14-18, 2017.

Gillespie, T. Becoming your own expert: Teachers as Writers. *The Quarterly*, 8(1), 1-2, 1985.

Goldschmied, E., Forbes, R., & Jackson, S. (2004). *People Under Three, Young Children in Day Care* (rev 3rd ed.). New York, NY: Routledge, 2014.

Goodman, Y., & Altwerger, B. Print awareness in preschool children: A study of the development of literacy in preschool children. Occasional paper number 4, Program in language and literacy, Arizona Center for Research and Development, College of Education, University of Arizona, 1981.

Graham, S., Gillespie, A., & McKeown, D. Writing: Importance, development, and instruction. *Reading & Writing*, 26(1), 1-15, 2013.

Hall, N. Play, literacy, and the role of the teacher. In J. R. Moyles (Ed.), *The Excellence of Play* (pp. 113-124). Philadelphia, PA: Open University Press, 1994.

Harste, J., Burke, C., & Woodward, V. Children's language and world: Initial encounters with print. In J.A. Langer & M.T. Smith-Burke (Eds.), *Reader Meets Author/Bridging the Gap: A Psycholinguistic Perspective* (pp. 105-131). Newark, DE: International Reading Association, 1982.

Hayes, A. From scribbling to writing: Smoothing the way. *Young Children*, 45(3), 62-68, 1990.

Heath, S. *Ways with Words: Language, Life, and Word in Communities and Classrooms.* New York: Cambridge University Press, 1983.

Heroman, C. & Copple, C. Teaching in the kindergarten year. In Dominic F. Gullo (Ed.) *K Today: Teaching and Learning in the Kindergarten Year.* Washington, DC: National Association for the Education of Young Children, 2006.

Hiebert, E.H. Preschool children's understanding of written language. *Child Development*, 49(4), 1231-1234, 1978.

Hill, Mary. *Signs on the Road.* (Signs in My World Series) New York, NY. Scholastic, 1977.

Hoban, Tana. *I Read Signs.* New York, NY. Harper Collins, 1983.

Hoban, Tana. *I Read Symbols.* New York, NY. Harper Collins, 1983.

Horner, S.L. Categories of environmental print: All logos are not created equal. *Early Childhood Education Journal*, 33(2), 113-119, 2005.

Bibliography

Hyvonen, P. T. Play in the school context? The perspectives of Finnish teachers. *Australian Journal of Teacher Education*, 36(8), 65–83, 2011.

Johnson, Stephen T. *A is for Art: An Abstract Alphabet*. New York, NY. Simon & Schuster, 2008.

Kassow, D.Z. Environmental print awareness in young children. *Talaris Research Institute*, 1(3), 1-8, 2006.

Kessen, W., & Mussen, P. H. Piaget's Theory. In William S. Damon and Richard Lerner (Eds.) *Handbook of Child Psychology: Vol. 1, History, Theory, and Methods*. New York, NY: Wiley, 1983.

Kettenring, L., & Graybill, N. Cereal boxes foster emergent literacy. *The Reading Teacher*, 44(7) 522-523, 1991.

Kirkland, L., Aldridge, J., & Kuby, P. Environmental print and the kindergarten classroom. *Reading Improvement*, 28(4), 219-222, 1991.

Kuby, P., Aldridge, J., & Snyder, S. Developmental progression of environmental print recognition in kindergarten classroom. *Reading Psychology: An International Quarterly*, 15, 1-9, 1994.

Kuby, P., Kirkland, L., & Aldridge, J. Learning about environmental print through picture books. *Early Childhood Education Journal*, 24(1), 33-36, 1996.

Lillard, A. S., Pinkham, A., & Smith, E.D. Pretend play and cognitive development. In U. Goswami (Ed.), *The Wiley-Blackwell Handbook of Childhood Cognitive Development* (pp. 285–311). Chichester, England: Wiley, 2011.

Lindqvist, G. When small children play: How adults dramatise and children create meaning. *Early Years*, 21, 7-14, 2001.

McEntee, G. H. Diving with Whales: Five Reasons for Practitioners to Write for Publication. *The Quarterly*, 20(4), 21-26, 1998.

McGee, L.M., & Jones, C. Learning to use print in the environment: A collaboration. *The Reading Teacher*, 44, 170–172, 1990.

McGee, L.M., & Richgels, D.J. *Literacy's Beginnings: Supporting Young Readers and Writers* (3rd ed.). Boston, MA: Allyn & Bacon, 2000.

Meier, D. *The Power of their Ideas: Lessons for America from a Small School in Harlem*. Boston, MA: Beacon Press, 1995.

Miller, E. & Almon, J. *Crisis in the Kindergarten: Why We Need Play in Schools*. College Park, MD: Alliance for Childhood, 2009.

Morrow, L. M. Preparing the classroom environment to promote literacy during play. *Early Childhood Research Quarterly*, 5(4), 537-554, 1990.

Morrow, L. M. Story Retelling: A discussion strategy to develop and assess comprehension. In Gambrell, L. B. & Almasi, 1. F. (Eds.), *Lively Discussions! Fostering Engaged Reading* (pp. 265-285). Newark, DE: International Reading Association, 1996.

Morrow, L. M. *Literacy Development in the Early Years: Helping Children Learn to Read and Write* (4th ed.). Boston, MA: Allyn & Bacon, 2000.

Morrow, L. M. *Literacy Development in the Early Years: Helping Children Read and Write* (7th ed.). Upper Saddle River, NJ: Pearson, 2011.

Mundy, P., Sigman, M., Ungerer, J., & Sherman, T. Nonverbal communication and play correlates of language development in autistic children. *Journal of Autism and Developmental Disorders*, 17(3), 349-364, 1987.

Neuman, S. B., & Roskos, K. Play, print and purpose: Enriching play environments for literacy development. *The Reading Teacher*, 44(3), 214-221, 1990.

Neuman, S., & Roskos, K. Peers as literacy informants: a description of young children's literacy conversations in play. *Early Childhood Research Quarterly*, 6(2):233-248, 1991.

Neuman, S., & Roskos, K. Play settings as literacy environments: Their effects on children's literacy behaviors. (pp.251-264) In Lancy, David F. (Ed.) *Childrens Emergent Literacy: From Research to Practice*. Praeger Publishers, Westport, CT: 1994.

Neuman, S. B., & Roskos, K. Whatever happened to developmentally appropriate practices in literacy? *Young Children*, 60, 1–6, 2005.

Nourot, P. M., & Van Hoorn, J. L. Symbolic play in preschool and primary settings. *Young Children*, 54, 40-47, 1991.

Oken-Wright, P. Transition to writing: Drawing as a scaffold for emergent writers. *Young Children*, 53(2), 76-81, 1998.

Ouellette, G., & Sénéchal, M. Invented spelling in kindergarten as a predictor of reading and spelling in Grade 1: A new pathway to literacy, or just the same road, less known? *Developmental Psychology*, 53(1), 77-88, 2017.

Owocki. G. *Literacy Through Play*. Portsmouth, NH: Heinemann, 1999.

Pellegrini, A. D. Relations between preschool children's symbolic play and literate behavior (pp. 79-97). In L. Galda & A. D. Pellegrini (Eds.) *Play, Language, and Stories: The Development of Literate Behavior*. Norwood, NJ: Ablex, 1985.

Piaget, J. *Play, Dreams and Imitation in Childhood*. New York, NY: Norton, 1962.

Purcell-Gates, V. Stories, coupons, and the TV Guide: Relationship between home literacy experiences and emergent literacy knowledge. *Reading Research Quarterly*, 31(4), 406-428, 1996.

Read, C. Children's Categorization of Speech Sounds in English. Urbana, IL: ERIC Clearinghouse on Reading and Communication Skills. ED 112 426, 1975.

Reutzel, D.R., Fawson, P.C., Young, J.R., Morrison, T.G., & Wilcox, B. Reading environmental print: What is the role of concepts about print in discriminating young readers' responses? *Reading Psychology*, 24(2), 123-162, 2003.

Rog, L. *Guided Reading Basics: Organizing, Managing, and Implementing a Balanced Literacy Program* in K-3. Portsmouth, NH: Stenhouse Publishers, 2002.

Roskos, K. *Creating Connections, Building Constructions: Language, Literacy, and Play in Early Childhood*. Newark, DE: International Reading Association, 2000.

Roskos, K. & Neuman, S. Play settings as literacy environments: Their effects on children's literacy behaviors. (pp.251-264) In Lancy, David F. (Ed.) *Childrens Emergent Literacy: From Research to Practice*. Westport, CT: Praeger Publishers, 1994.

Routman, R. Transitions: *From Literature to Literacy*. Portsmouth, NH: Heinemann, 1991.

Rule, A. C. Alphabetizing with environmental print. *The Reading Teacher*, 54(6), 558-562, 2001.

Schickedanz, J. A. *More Than the ABCs: The Early Stages of Reading and Writing.* Washington, DC: National Association for the Education of Young Children, 1986.

Schickedanz, J. A. *Much More Than ABC's: The Early Stages of Reading and Writing.* Washington, DC: National Association for the Education of Young Children, 1999.

Schickedanz, J. A., & Casbergue, R. *Writing in Preschool: Learning to Orchestrate Meaning and Marks.* Newark, NJ: International Reading Association, 2004.

Schultze, B. *Basic Tools for Beginning Writers: How to Teach All the Skills Beginning Writers Need—From Alphabet Recognition and Spelling to Strategies for Self-Editing and Building Coherent Text.* Portsmouth, NH: Stenhouse Publishers, 2008.

Shaffer, G., & McNinch, G. Parents' perceptions of young children's awareness of environmental print. In W. Linek & E. Sturtevant (Eds.), *Generations of Literacy: The Seventeenth Yearbook of the College Reading Association* (pp. 278-286). Washington, DC: National Academy Press, 1995.

Shore, C., O'Connell, B., & Bates, E. First sentences in language and symbolic play. *Developmental Psychology*, 20, 872-880, 1984.

Skolnick D, Ilgaz H, Hirsh-Pasek K, et al. (2015) Shovels and swords: How realistic and fantastical themes affect children's word learning. *Cognitive Development* (35): 1–14.

Snow, C.M., Burns, M., & Griffin, P. (Eds.). *Preventing Reading Difficulties in Young Children.* Washington, DC: National Academy Press, 1998.

Stagnitti, K., & Lewis, F. M. Quality of pre-school children's pretend play and subsequent development of semantic organization and narrative re-telling skills. *International Journal of Speech-Language Pathology*, 17(2), 148-58, 2015.

Strickland, D. S. & Morrow, L. M. Environments rich in print promote literacy behavior during play. *Reading Teacher*, 43(4), 330-331, 1998.

Stroud, J.E. Block play: Building a foundation for literacy. *Early Childhood Education Journal*, 23(1), 9-13, 1995.

Bibliography

Sulzby, E. Research directions: Transitions from emergent to conventional writing. *Language Arts*, 69(4), 290-97, 1992.

Sutherland, S., & Friedman, O. Just pretending can be really learning: Children use pretend play as a source for acquiring generic knowledge. *Developmental Psychology*, 49(9), 1660-1668, 2013.

Taylor, J., Branscombe, N., Burcham, J., & Land, L. *Beyond Early Literacy: A Balanced Approach to Developing the Whole Child*. New York, NY: Routledge, 2010.

Teale, W.H. Home background and young children's literacy development. 1986. In W.H. Teale & E. Sulzby (Eds.) *Emergent Literacy: Reading and Writing*. Norwood, NJ: Ablex, 1996.

Temple, C., Nathan, R., Temple, F., & Burris, N. *The Beginnings of Writing* (3rd ed.). Boston, MA: Allyn & Bacon, 1993.

The National Commission on Writing in America's Schools and Colleges. *The Neglected "R": The Need for a Writing Revolution*. Princeton, NJ: College Entrance Examination Board, 2003.

Thompkins, G. E. *Teaching Writing: Balancing Process and Product*. Upper Saddle River, NJ: Pearson, 2004.

Tunks, K. W., Giles, R. M. *Write now! Publishing with Young Authors: Pre-K through Grade 2*. Portsmouth, NH: Heinemann, 2007

Tunks, K. W., Giles, R. M. Writing their words: Strategies for supporting young authors. *Young Children*, 64(1), 22-25, 2009.

Vukelich, C. & Valentine, C. A child plays: Two teachers learn. *Reading Teacher*, 44(4), 342-344, 1990.

Vukelich, C. Where's the paper? Literacy during dramatic play. *Childhood Education*, 67, 205-209, 1990.

Vukelich, C. Effects of play interventions on young children's reading of environmental print. *Early Childhood Research Quarterly*, 9, 153-170, 1994.

Vygotsky, L. S. (1933). The role of play in development. In M. Cole, V. John-Steiner, S. (Eds.), *Mind in Society* (p 92-104). Cambridge, MA: Harvard University Press, 1980.

Vygotsky, L. S. Play and its role in the mental development of the child. *Soviet Psychology*, 12, 67-76, 1966.

Weininger, O. *Play and Education: The Basic Tool for Early Childhood Learning.* Springfield, IL: Charles C. Thomas, 1979.

Weisberg, D. S., Zosh, J. M., Hirsh-Pasek, K., & Golinkoff, R. M. Talking it up: Play, language development, and the role adult support. *American Journal of Play*, 6(1), 39-54, 2013.

Weitzman, E. *Learning Language and Loving It.* Toronto, Ontario: Hanen Center, 1992.

Wilson, R.A. *Special educational needs in the early years* (2nd edition). New York, NY: Routledge, 2003.

Wollman-Bonilla, J. *Family Message Journals: Teaching Writing Through Family Involvement.* Urbana, IL: National Council of Teachers of English, 2000.

Work, B. (Ed) *Learning Through the Eyes of a Child: A Guide to Best Teaching Practices in Early Education.* Raleigh, NC: North Carolina State Department of Public Instruction, 2002.

Bibliography

ABOUT THE AUTHOR

Dr. Rebecca McMahon Giles is a Professor in the Department of Leadership and Teacher Education at the University of South Alabama in Mobile, AL where she teaches courses in the undergraduate Early Childhood Studies program as well as the graduate Elementary and Early Childhood Education programs. She received her M.Ed. from the University of Texas at Austin and her Ph.D. from the University of Southern Mississippi. She has taught prekindergarten, kindergarten, and first grade in both public and private school settings and has over 25 years of experience in higher education. Dr. Giles has spoken and published widely on a variety of early childhood topics and is co-author of *Write Now! Publishing with Young Authors, PreK through Grade 2* (Heinemann, 2007). She lives in Ocean Springs, MS with her husband Bryan and teenage sons, Jay and Kade.

www.ingramcontent.com/pod-product-compliance
Lightning Source LLC
Chambersburg PA
CBHW061138230426
43662CB00023B/2463